Better Homes and Gardens

CROCKERY COOKBOOK

BETTER HOMES AND GARDENS® BOOKS
An Imprint of Meredith® Books
President, Book Group: Joseph J. Ward
Vice President and Editorial Director: Elizabeth P. Rice
Managing Editor: Christopher Cavanaugh
Art Director: Ernest Shelton
Test Kitchen Director: Sharon Stilwell

Crockery Cookbook
Editor: Lisa L. Mannes
Contributing Editor: Marla Mason
Graphic Designer: Lynda Haupert
Test Kitchen Product Supervisor: Jennifer Peterson
Food Stylist: Janet Pittman
Cover Photographer: Mike Dieter
Production Manager: Douglas Johnston
Production Editor: Paula Forest

On the cover: Chunky Vegetable Chili, page 97

All of us at Better Homes and Gardens® Books are dedicated
to providing you with the information and ideas you need to
create tasty foods. We welcome your comments and suggestions.
Write us at: Better Homes and Gardens® Books,
Cookbook Editorial Department, LN112, 1716 Locust Street,
Des Moines, IA 50309-3023

Our seal assures you that every recipe in Crockery Cookbook
has been tested in the Better Homes and Gardens® Test Kitchen.
This means that each recipe is practical and reliable, and meets
our high standards of taste appeal. We guarantee your satisfaction
with this book for as long as you own it.

Introduction

*Crowded schedules make our lives hectic and
leave each of us looking for ways to make our day
a little easier. The crockery cooker is one
appliance that helps to simplify cooking and
make our favorite dishes more feasible.*

*Whether you're working full-time or in the
home, running errands or preparing to entertain guests,
the crockery cooker virtually eliminates
the last-minute panic of mealtime preparation. By
choosing the low-heat or high-heat setting, you
can adjust your cooker to your meal schedule and
have every meal ready when you are.*

Contents

Types of Crockery Cookers

There are two basic types of crockery cookers (see illustrations, A and B). Recipes for this book were tested only in the type shown in Illustration A. This type of cooker has a crockery insert and two temperature settings, low (about 200° F) and high (about 300° F). (One hour on high equals approximately 2 hours on low.) The heating element is coiled around the sides of the cooker surrounding the crockery insert. This allows for the continuous slow cooking needed for the recipes in this book.

The cooker in Illustration B has an adjustable thermostat, indicating temperature in degrees. The heating element is located in the bottom of the cooker allowing heat to be applied only at the bottom of the container. Since the heating element cycles on and off, our recipes will not work in this type of cooker.

Since the midsize crockery cookers are the most popular, the recipes in this book were tested in 3½-, 4-, 5-, and 6-quart models.

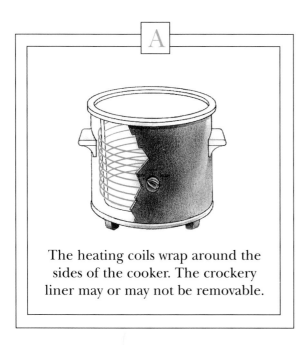

A

The heating coils wrap around the sides of the cooker. The crockery liner may or may not be removable.

B

The heating coil is below the container.

Tips for Using Your Crockery Cooker

As with any appliance, it is best to read the manufacturer's use and care booklet for specific instructions when using your crockery cooker. The following tips are general guidelines you might find helpful when using your crockery cooker.

If you plan to leave early in the morning, start your preparations the previous night. Place cleaned and chopped vegetables, seasonings, and liquids into a bowl or the crockery liner if it is removable. Chill the vegetables. The following morning, assemble all ingredients in the cooker, cover, and spend the rest of the day as you like.

There may be times when you will be gone a little longer than the recipe needs to cook. In these instances you might want to use an automatic timer to start your cooker. These can be purchased at a hardware store.

When using the automatic timer, prepare the recipe and thoroughly chill all ingredients. When you're ready to leave, fill the cooker, plug it into the timer, set the timer, and turn on the cooker. It is important to remember the food should never stand more than two hours before it begins cooking. We also do not recommend this method for recipes that include frozen fish.

Resist the temptation to lift the lid during cooking. Removing the lid, even for a moment, allows significant amounts of heat to escape and extends the cooking time. Because the crockery cooker cooks at such low temperatures, it is unable to quickly recover the lost heat and return to the desired temperature. When instructed to lift the lid near the end of cooking time, do so quickly and efficiently, replacing the lid as soon as possible.

For food safety, remove any leftover food from the crockery cooker as soon as possible. Place the leftovers in a storage container and refrigerate or freeze (see page 10).

The best way to clean your crockery cooker is to follow your manufacturer's guidelines. Always remember to unplug your cooker before cleaning and never immerse the cooker or cord in water. Also, to avoid cracking the crockery insert, add only warm water if the unit is still hot.

Adapting Recipes

By following a few guidelines you can adapt your own favorite recipes to the crockery cooker.

 Start by finding a similar recipe in this book. This gives you an idea of quantities, amounts of liquids, and times needed to cook the recipe.

 It is generally not necessary to sauté the vegetables first. Simply chop or cut them into bite-size pieces and place them in the bottom of your cooker.

 Since the low, moist heat of the crockery cooker is ideal for tenderizing less expensive cuts of meats, you can save the more expensive ones for roasting or grilling. Select a size that will fit into your cooker. Trim away as much visible fat as possible, brown, and place atop vegetables.

 Because liquids do not boil away as in conventional cooking, reduce the amount of liquid in your favorite recipe by approximately one-half. The exception would be soups and those recipes containing long grain converted rice.

 Dairy products such as milk, creams, and natural cheeses tend to break down during extended cooking. Condensed soups and nonfat dry milk powder can be mixed and substituted for milk or cream. Evaporated milk can be added during the last 30 to 60 minutes of cooking time. If you prefer, stir cream, sour cream, or cheese into the cooker just before serving. For a smoother sauce, add a small amount of the hot cooking liquid to the cream or sour cream first, and then add to the cooker.

Reducing Fats

The low, moist heat of the crockery cooker lends itself well to cooking with very little fat. With this in mind, choose lean cuts of meat, trimming away as much visible fat as possible. For poultry, remove the skin before cooking. Try browning the meat in a non-stick skillet sprayed with a nonstick coating instead of browning in cooking oil.

To skim the fat before serving, use a slotted spoon to transfer the meat and vegetables to a serving platter. Pour the cooking liquid into a glass measuring cup and let stand a minute or two to allow the fat to rise to the top. Skim off any visible fat with a spoon.

Making Foil Handles

Foil handles make it easy to lift a soufflé dish or meat loaf out of the crockery cooker. To make, tear off three 18 x 2-inch strips of heavy foil or use regular foil folded to double thickness. Crisscross the foil strips in a spoke design. (Place on a large sheet of waxed paper if shaping meat loaf.) Place the soufflé dish or shaped meat loaf in the center of the spoke.

Lift the ends of the foil strips to transfer the dish or meat loaf to the cooker (see illustration right). Leave the strips under the dish or meat during cooking for easy removal. When ready to serve, lift the dish or meat from the cooker with the foil handles.

Freezing and Reheating Leftovers

If you're left with extra servings at the end of your meal, follow these suggestions for freezing and reheating the food.

To properly freeze liquid or semiliquid foods, select appropriate packaging such as wide-mouth freezing or canning jars, rigid plastic freezer containers with tight fitting lids, and freezer bags. Leave enough head-space in the container for the food to expand as it freezes. On wide-mouth containers leave ½-inch for pints and 1 inch for quarts; on narrow-mouth containers leave ¾-inch for pints and 1½-inches for quarts.

Although foods may be stored for a long time in the freezer, they won't keep forever. Soups, stews, and meat with gravy may be frozen for 1 to 3 months. Keep in mind that some vegetables freeze better than others; potatoes tend to be dry and crumbly after freezing, but they are edible.

To reheat stews and soups, place the frozen mixture in a heavy saucepan. Cook over low heat, stirring the mixture often with a fork until thoroughly heated. Meat dishes with gravy should be thawed overnight in the refrigerator before reheating.

To reheat frozen soup in the microwave, cook on 70% power (medium-high heat) and allow about 7 minutes for 1 cup, 12 minutes for 2 cups, and 20 minutes for 3 cups. For a frozen stewlike mixture, allow about 5 minutes for 1 cup, 9 minutes for 2 cups, and 14 minutes for 3 cups. For a combination similar to roast beef and gravy, allow about 11 minutes for 1 cup, 16 minutes for 2 cups, and 20 minutes for 3 cups.

Appetizers & Beverages

❦

Tangy Cocktail Meatballs

*If stuffing mix is unavailable, use croutons and lightly crush them with a
rolling pin or the bottom of a mixing bowl.*

1   **beaten egg**
1   **10½-ounce can condensed French onion
     soup**
2   **cups herb-seasoned stuffing mix**
½   **teaspoon seasoned salt**
2   **pounds ground beef**

1   **cup salsa-style catsup or regular catsup**
1   **8-ounce can tomato sauce**
1   **cup water**
⅓   **cup packed brown sugar**
¼   **cup Worcestershire sauce**
¼   **cup vinegar**
2   **tablespoons quick-cooking tapioca**

1 In a large bowl combine egg, soup, stuffing mix, and salt. Add ground beef; mix well. Shape into 1-inch meatballs. Place meatballs in a 15x10x1-inch baking pan. Bake in a 350° oven for 15 to 18 minutes or till done. Drain meatballs and transfer to a 3½-, 4-, or 5-quart crockery cooker.

2 In a bowl combine catsup, tomato sauce, water, brown sugar, Worcestershire sauce, vinegar, and tapioca. Pour over meatballs; stir gently to coat.

3 Cover; cook on high-heat setting for 2 to 3 hours. Serve immediately or keep warm on low-heat setting up to 2 hours. Serve with toothpicks. Makes about 50 meatballs.

Per meatball: 58 calories, 4 g protein, 5 g carbohydrate, 3 g total fat (1 g saturated), 15 mg cholesterol, 191 mg sodium, 101 mg potassium

Spicy Sausage Pizza Dip

Surprise your party guests with their favorite pizza flavors—served up in a spicy dip.

1 **pound bulk Italian sausage**
1 **small onion, chopped (⅓ cup)**
2 **cloves garlic, minced**

1 **15-ounce can tomato sauce**
1 **7½-ounce can tomatoes, cut up**
½ **of a 6-ounce can tomato paste (⅓ cup)**
2 **teaspoons dried oregano, crushed**
1½ **teaspoons dried basil, crushed**
1 **teaspoon sugar**
⅛ **teaspoon ground red pepper**

¼ **cup chopped black olives**
2 **tablespoons grated Parmesan cheese**
   Dippers: breadsticks, breaded
      mozzarella cheese sticks, and green
      sweet pepper strips

1 In a large skillet cook Italian sausage, onion, and garlic till meat is brown and onion is tender; drain well.

2 In a 3½- or 4-quart crockery cooker combine sausage mixture, tomato sauce, *undrained* tomatoes, tomato paste, oregano, basil, sugar, and red pepper. Stir all ingredients together. Cover; cook on low-heat setting for 6 to 8 hours or on high-heat setting for 3 to 4 hours.

3 Stir in olives. Sprinkle with grated Parmesan cheese. Serve with desired dippers. Makes 3½ cups dip.

Per serving: 106 calories, 6 g protein, 6 g carbohydrate, 7 g total fat (2 g saturated), 19 mg cholesterol, 472 mg sodium, 298 mg potassium.

Barbecue-Style Chicken Wings

Vary the flavor of this party-starter by choosing your favorite style barbecue sauce.
Be sure to have plenty of napkins on hand!

3 pounds chicken wings (about 16)

1½ cups bottled barbecue sauce
¼ cup honey
2 teaspoons prepared mustard
1½ teaspoons Worcestershire sauce

1 Rinse chicken; pat dry. Cut off and discard wing tips. Cut each wing at joint to make 2 sections.

2 Place chicken on the unheated rack of a broiler pan. Broil 4 to 5 inches from the heat about 10 minutes or till chicken is browned, turning once. Transfer chicken to a 3½- or 4-quart crockery cooker.

3 For sauce, combine barbecue sauce, honey, mustard, and Worcestershire sauce; pour over chicken wings. Cover; cook on low-heat setting for 4 to 5 hours or on high-heat setting for 2 to 2½ hours. Makes about 32 appetizers.

Per appetizer: 67 calories, 5 g protein, 4 g carbohydrate, 4 g total fat (1 g saturated), 14 mg cholesterol, 115 mg sodium, 52 mg potassium

Sweet 'n' Sour Hamballs

Cocktail wieners or Polish sausage pieces would make a nice variation.

1 **9- or 10-ounce bottle sweet and sour sauce**
⅓ **cup unsweetened pineapple juice**
⅓ **cup packed brown sugar**
¼ **teaspoon ground ginger**

1 **beaten egg**
½ **cup graham cracker crumbs**
2 **tablespoons milk**
½ **pound ground fully cooked ham**
½ **pound ground pork**
   Nonstick spray coating

1 In a 3½- or 4-quart crockery cooker stir together sweet and sour sauce, pineapple juice, brown sugar, and ground ginger. Set aside.

2 For meatballs, in a large bowl combine egg, graham cracker crumbs, and milk. Add ground ham and pork; mix well. Shape into 30 meatballs. Spray a 12-inch skillet with nonstick coating. Add meatballs and brown on all sides over medium heat.

3 Add browned meatballs to crockery cooker. Cover; cook on low-heat setting for 4 to 5 hours or on high-heat setting for 1½ to 2 hours. Serve immediately or keep warm on low-heat setting for up to 2 hours. Makes 30 meatballs.

Per meatball: *51 calories, 3 g protein, 7 g carbohydrate, 1g total fat (0 g saturated), 13 mg cholesterol, 130 mg sodium, 63 mg potassium*

Tex-Mex Cheese Dip

*Spice up this Mexican-style dip with hot salsa and use
sausage instead of ground beef.*

1½ **pounds lean ground beef or ground
    raw chicken or raw turkey**
1 **cup chopped onion**
2 **cloves garlic, minced**

1 **teaspoon ground cumin**
1 **teaspoon ground coriander**
1 **12-ounce jar chunky salsa**

1 **16-ounce package cheese spread with
    jalapeño peppers, shredded
    Tortilla chips or corn chips**

1 In a skillet cook beef, chicken, or turkey,
onion, and garlic till meat is brown. Drain
off fat.

2 Transfer meat mixture to a 3½- or 4-quart
crockery cooker. Stir in cumin, coriander,
and salsa. Cover; cook on low-heat setting
for 3 to 4 hours or on high-heat setting for
1½ to 2 hours till heated through.

3 Stir in cheese. Cover; cook on high-heat
setting for 5 to 10 minutes or till cheese
melts. Serve with chips. The dip may be kept
warm in crockery cooker up to 2 hours on
low-heat setting. Makes about 6 cups.

*Per ¼ cup dip without chips: 133 calories, 10 g pro-
tein, 2 g carbohydrate, 10 g total fat (1 g saturated),
36 mg cholesterol, 341 mg sodium, 125 mg potassium*

Cranberry-Sauced Franks

*Vary the hotness of this recipe with different styles of barbecue sauce. Or, try
using pieces of frankfurters or Polish sausages for a change of pace.*

2 1-pound packages cocktail wieners

1 cup chili sauce
1 cup bottled barbecue sauce
1 8-ounce can jellied cranberry sauce

1 Place cocktail wieners in a 3½- or 4-quart crockery cooker.

2 For sauce, combine chili sauce, barbecue sauce, and cranberry sauce. Pour over wieners.

3 Cover; cook on low-heat setting for 3 to 4 hours or on high-heat setting for 1½ to 2 hours. Serve immediately or keep warm on low-heat setting for up to 2 hours. Serve with a slotted spoon or toothpicks. Makes 32 servings.

Per serving: 114 calories, 4 g protein, 7 g carbohydrate, 8 g total fat (3 g saturated), 15 mg cholesterol, 441 mg sodium, 91 mg potassium

Five-Spice Pecans

The slow cooker gently toasts these Oriental-inspired nuts. Make extra
ahead and freeze—then give as holiday gifts.

1 pound pecan halves (4 cups)
¼ cup margarine or butter, melted
2 tablespoons soy sauce
1 teaspoon five-spice powder
½ teaspoon garlic powder
½ teaspoon ground ginger
¼ teaspoon ground red pepper

1 Place pecans in a 3½- or 4-quart crockery cooker. In a bowl combine the melted margarine or butter, soy sauce, five-spice powder, garlic powder, ginger, and red pepper. Pour over nuts. Stir to coat nuts.

2 Cover; cook on low-heat setting for 2 hours. Uncover and stir. Turn to high-heat setting. Cover and continue cooking on high-heat setting for 15 to 30 minutes. Cool. Makes about 4 cups.

Per ¼ cup serving: 217 calories, 2 g protein, 6 g carbo-hydrate, 22 g total fat (3 g saturated), 8 mg choles-terol, 145 mg sodium, 120 mg potassium

Spicy Tomato Cocktail

A perfect starter for your next brunch or tailgate party.

1 **46-ounce can vegetable juice**
1 **stalk celery, halved (if necessary to fit)**
2 **tablespoons brown sugar**
2 **tablespoons lemon juice**
1½ **teaspoons prepared horseradish**
1 **teaspoon Worcestershire sauce**
½ **teaspoon bottled hot pepper sauce**

Lemon slices, halved (optional)

1 In a 3½- or 4-quart crockery cooker combine vegetable juice, celery, brown sugar, lemon juice, horseradish, Worcestershire sauce, and hot pepper sauce.

2 Cover; cook on low-heat setting for 3 to 4 hours or on high-heat setting for 1 to 1½ hours. Discard celery. Ladle beverage into cups and float a lemon half slice atop each serving, if desired. Makes 8 (6-ounce) servings.

Per serving: 47 calories, 1 g protein, 12 g carbohydrate, 0 g total fat (0 g saturated), 0 mg cholesterol, 612 mg sodium, 359 mg potassium

Party Time with your Cooker

When it's cold and damp outside, greet your guests with the enticing aroma of a spiced cocktail simmering in your crockery cooker. On the low-heat setting, your hot beverage will stay a perfect sipping temperature throughout the party.

And because your guests can serve themselves from the cooker, you will save on replenishing trips back and forth to the range-top.

Mulled Cider

Use the processed cider found on the grocery shelf. The unprocessed cider found in the supermarket's refrigerated section will separate and have a curdled appearance when heated.

Peel from ½ orange, cut into pieces
6 **inches stick cinnamon, broken***
1 **1-inch piece gingerroot, peeled and thinly sliced**
1 **teaspoon whole allspice**

8 **cups apple cider or apple juice**
1 **cup apple brandy (optional)**
¼ **cup honey or packed brown sugar**

1 For spice bag, cut a double thickness of 100 percent cotton cheesecloth into a 6- or 8-inch square. Place orange peel, cinnamon, gingerroot, and allspice in center of cheesecloth square. Bring up corners of cheesecloth and tie with a clean string.

2 In a 3½-, 4-, or 5-quart crockery cooker combine apple cider or apple juice, apple brandy (if desired), and honey or brown sugar. Add spice bag to cider mixture.

3 Cover; cook on low-heat setting for 5 to 6 hours or on high-heat setting for 2½ to 3 hours. Remove spice bag and discard. Ladle cider into cups. Makes 8 or 9 (8-ounce) servings.

***Note:** To break cinnamon sticks, place in a heavy plastic bag and pound sticks with a meat mallet.

***Per serving:** 149 calories, 0 g protein, 38 g carbohydrate, 0 g total fat (0 g saturated), 0 mg cholesterol, 8 mg sodium, 303 mg potassium*

Holiday Wassail

This fruity wassail is bound to become a holiday favorite.

6 inches stick cinnamon, broken
12 whole cloves

8 cups water
½ of a 12-ounce can frozen cranberry
    juice cocktail concentrate (¾ cup)
½ of a 12-ounce can frozen raspberry
    juice blend concentrate (¾ cup)
1 6-ounce can frozen apple juice concen-
    trate (¾ cup)
½ cup sugar
⅓ cup lemon juice

½ to ¾ cup brandy or rum or 6 tea bags
    (optional)

Orange slices (optional)

1 For spice bag, cut a double thickness of 100 percent cotton cheesecloth into a 6-inch square. Place cinnamon and cloves in center of cheesecloth square. Bring up corners of cheesecloth and tie with a clean string.

2 In a 3½-, 4-, or 5-quart crockery cooker combine water, cranberry juice cocktail concentrate, raspberry juice blend concentrate, apple juice concentrate, sugar, and lemon juice. Add the spice bag to juice mixture.

3 Cover; cook on low-heat setting for 5 to 6 hours or on high-heat setting for 2½ to 3 hours. Remove the spice bag and discard. If desired, about 5 minutes before serving, add brandy or rum or the tea bags to the crockery cooker. Allow to stand for 5 minutes. Discard the tea bags, if using.

4 To serve, ladle beverage into cups. If desired, float an orange slice atop each serving. Makes 14 (6-ounce) servings.

Per serving: *80 calories, 0 g protein, 21 g carbohydrate, 0 g total fat (0 g saturated), 0 mg cholesterol, 8 mg sodium, 102 mg potassium*

Chocolate Cream Cocoa

*Vary this rich and delicious drink by using different
flavored creamers and liqueurs.*

1 **9.6-ounce package nonfat dry milk
     powder (about 3½ cups)**
¾ **cup powdered sugar**
¾ **cup unsweetened cocoa powder**
¾ **cup Irish cream-flavored, powdered
     nondairy creamer or plain
     powdered nondairy creamer**
8 **cups water**

½ **cup creme de cacao (optional)
     Sweetened whipped cream**

1 In a 3½-, 4-, or 5-quart crockery cooker
combine dry milk powder, powdered sugar,
cocoa powder, and nondairy creamer.
Gradually add water; stir well to dissolve.

2 Cover; cook on low-heat setting for 3
to 4 hours or on high-heat setting for 1½
to 2 hours.

3 Stir in the creme de cacao, if desired.
Stir mixture before serving. Ladle into
mugs; top with whipped cream. Makes
about 12 (6-ounce) servings.

*Per serving: 214 calories, 9 g protein, 30 g carbohy-
drate, 7 g total fat (5 g saturated), 14 mg cholesterol,
147 mg sodium, 443 mg potassium*

Mulled Wine

*Since boiling wine makes it bitter, the crockery cooker is
a great way to make this classic drink.*

2 whole cardamom pods
16 whole cloves
3 inches stick cinnamon, broken (see
   note, page 20)

2 750-milliliter bottles dry red wine
2 cups water
1 cup light corn syrup

2 oranges, halved

Orange slices, halved (optional)
Cinnamon sticks (optional)

1 For spice bag, cut a double thickness of 100 percent cotton cheesecloth into a 5- or 6-inch square. Pinch cardamom pods to break open. Place cardamom, cloves, and cinnamon in center of cheesecloth square. Bring up corners of cheesecloth and tie with a clean string.

2 In a 3½-, 4-, or 5-quart crockery cooker combine wine, water, and corn syrup. Add spice bag.

3 Cover; cook on low-heat setting for 4 to 5 hours or on high-heat setting for 2 to 2½ hours. (Do not let boil.) Add orange halves the last ½ hour of cooking. Remove spice bag and orange halves and discard.

4 To serve, ladle beverage into cups. If desired, float a fresh orange slice atop each serving and add a cinnamon stick. Makes 12 (6-ounce) servings.

Per serving: 180 calories, 1 g protein, 25 g carbohydrate, 0 g total fat (0 g saturated), 0 mg cholesterol, 102 mg sodium, 236 mg potassium

Soups & Stews

Stewed Beef and Broth

*This rich broth is worth the extra effort. Use the cooked meat for barbecue
sandwiches or add it to soups, stews, or casseroles.*

3 pounds meaty beef soup bones
   (beef shank crosscuts or short ribs)
1 tablespoon cooking oil

2 large onions, sliced
4 cloves garlic, halved
8 sprigs parsley
4 large bay leaves
8 whole black peppercorns
1½ teaspoons salt
5 cups water

1 egg white (optional)
1 eggshell, crushed (optional)
¼ cup water (optional)

1 In a large skillet brown soup bones on all sides in hot oil.

2 In a 3½-, 4-, or 5-quart crockery cooker combine onions, garlic, parsley, bay leaves, peppercorns, and salt. Add soup bones and the 5 cups water.

3 Cover; cook on low-heat setting for 10 to 12 hours or on high-heat setting for 5 to 6 hours.

4 Remove bones from cooker. Strain broth through a large sieve or colander lined with 2 layers of 100 percent cotton cheesecloth. Discard solids in cheesecloth. If desired, clarify broth by combining egg white, eggshell, and ¼ cup water in a large saucepan. Add hot broth. Bring to boiling; let stand 5 minutes. Strain broth through 2 layers of 100 percent cotton cheesecloth.

5 If using broth right away, skim off fat. Or, if storing broth for later use, chill broth in a bowl for 6 hours. Lift off fat. Pour broth into an airtight container, discarding the residue in the bottom of the bowl; seal. Chill in the refrigerator for up to 3 days or freeze for up to 3 months.

6 When bones are cool enough to handle, remove meat from bones. Discard bones. Place the meat in an airtight container; seal. Chill in the refrigerator up to 3 days or freeze up to 3 months. Makes about 5½ cups broth and about 2½ cups cooked meat.

Per serving: *227 calories, 19 g protein, 8 g carbohydrate, 13 g total fat (5 g saturated), 53 mg cholesterol, 683 mg sodium, 307 mg potassium*

Stewed Chicken and Broth

This flavorful broth is lower in sodium than the canned version. Try it in any recipe that calls for chicken broth, especially chicken noodle soup.

4 to 4½ pounds of stewing, roasting, or broiler-fryer chicken, cut up
4 stalks celery with leaves, cut up
1 small onion, sliced
2 sprigs parsley
1 bay leaf
¾ teaspoon salt
½ teaspoon dried thyme or marjoram, crushed
¼ teaspoon pepper
4 cups cold water

1 In a 3½-, 4-, or 5-quart crockery cooker combine cut-up chicken, celery, onion, parsley, bay leaf, salt, thyme or marjoram, and pepper. Add water.

2 Cover; cook on low-heat setting for 7 to 10 hours or on high-heat setting for 3½ to 5 hours or till chicken is very tender and no longer pink.

3 Remove chicken from cooker. Strain broth through a large sieve or colander lined with 2 layers of 100 percent cotton cheesecloth. Discard solids in cheesecloth.

4 If using broth right away, skim off fat. Or, if storing broth for later use, chill broth in a bowl for 6 hours or overnight. Lift off fat. Pour broth into an airtight container; seal. Chill in the refrigerator for up to 3 days or freeze for up to 3 months.

5 When chicken is cool enough to handle, remove meat from bones. Discard skin and bones. Place meat in an airtight container; seal. Chill in the refrigerator up to 3 days or freeze up to 3 months. Makes about 5 cups broth and about 4 cups cooked meat.

Per serving: 264 calories, 24 g protein, 2 g carbohydrate, 17 g total fat (5 g saturated), 70 mg cholesterol, 296 mg sodium, 272 mg potassium

Zesty Beef and Vegetable Soup

Soup lovers can't resist this combination of spicy tomato base, beef, and vegetables. Complete the meal with cheesy corn bread.

1 **pound ground beef**
½ **cup chopped onion**
2 **cloves garlic, minced**

2 **cups pre-shredded coleslaw mix**
1 **10-ounce package frozen whole kernel corn**
1 **9-ounce package frozen cut green beans**
4 **cups hot-style vegetable juice**
1 **14½-ounce can Italian-style stewed tomatoes**
2 **tablespoons Worcestershire sauce**
1 **teaspoon dried basil, crushed**
¼ **teaspoon pepper**

1 In a large skillet cook ground beef, onion, and garlic till meat is brown and onion is tender. Drain off fat.

2 In a 3½-, 4-, or 5-quart crockery cooker combine meat mixture, coleslaw mix, frozen corn, frozen beans, vegetable juice, *undrained* tomatoes, Worcestershire sauce, basil, and pepper.

3 Cover; cook on low-heat setting for 8 to 10 hours or on high-heat setting for 4 to 5 hours. Makes 6 servings.

Per serving: 269 calories, 19 g protein, 29 g carbohydrate, 10 g total fat (4 g saturated), 48 mg cholesterol, 925 mg sodium, 972 mg potassium

Hearty Lamb and Barley Soup

*Look for lean lamb at the supermarket or buy
extra (2½ pounds) and trim it yourself. Beef and pork make
delicious substitutions for the lamb as well.*

1½ **pounds lamb stew meat, cut into
       1-inch cubes**
1 **tablespoon cooking oil**

2 **cups sliced fresh mushrooms**
½ **cup pearl barley**
1 **cup chopped onion**
1 **medium carrot, cut into ½-inch pieces**
1 **large parsnip, peeled and cut into
       ½-inch pieces**
1 **14½-ounce can Italian-style stewed
       tomatoes**
2 **cloves garlic, minced**
1 **teaspoon dried marjoram, crushed**
½ **teaspoon salt**
¼ **teaspoon pepper**
1 **bay leaf**
5 **cups beef broth (see tip, page 29)**

1 In a large skillet brown lamb, *half* at a
time, in hot oil. Drain off fat.

2 In a 3½-, 4-, or 5-quart crockery cooker
place meat, mushrooms, barley, onion,
carrot, parsnip, *undrained* tomatoes, garlic,
marjoram, salt, pepper, and bay leaf. Pour
beef broth over all.

3 Cover; cook on low-heat setting for 8 to
10 hours or on high-heat setting for 4 to 5
hours. Discard bay leaf. Makes 8 servings.

*Per serving: 255 calories, 17 g protein, 21 g carbohy-
drate, 12 g total fat (5 g saturated), 48 mg cholesterol,
854 mg sodium, 639 mg potassium*

Split Pea and Ham Soup

Smoked turkey sausage can be used in place of the ham.

2 **cups cubed fully cooked ham**
1 **cup dry split peas**
1 **cup chopped onion**
1 **cup chopped celery with leaves**
1 **cup shredded carrot**
2 **tablespoons snipped fresh parsley**
½ **teaspoon dried thyme, crushed**
¼ **teaspoon pepper**
4 **cups chicken broth (see tip on left side of page)**
2 **cups water**

1 **cup quick-cooking rice**

1 In a 3½-, 4-, or 5-quart crockery cooker combine ham, peas, onion, celery, carrot, parsley, thyme, and pepper. Pour chicken broth and water over all.

2 Cover; cook on low-heat setting for 10 to 12 hours or on high-heat setting for 4 to 5 hours. Stir in rice. Cover; let stand 5 minutes or till rice is tender. Makes 6 servings.

Per serving: 256 calories, 21 g protein, 35 g carbohydrate, 4 g total fat (1 g saturated), 15 mg cholesterol, 1,097 mg sodium, 701 mg potassium

Convenient Substitutes

When a recipe calls for beef broth, chicken broth, or vegetable broth, you can, if you like, make homemade broth using your crockery cooker and one of the recipes on pages 25, 26, and 92.

But if you're in a hurry, don't despair. Excellent broth substitutes are available. And if you don't have the flavor specified in the recipe, use a different one—you might even like it better!

Canned chicken and beef broth are ready to use straight from the can. Instant bouillon granules and cubes can be purchased in beef, chicken, vegetable, and onion flavors. One cube or 1 teaspoon of granules mixed with 1 cup water makes an easy broth.

Chicken and Vegetable Bean Soup

*This hearty recipe can easily be made into a great meatless
version by omitting the chicken.*

1 cup dry great northern beans
6 cups water

1 cup chopped onion
1 medium fennel bulb, trimmed and cut
     into ½-inch pieces
2 medium carrots, chopped
2 cloves garlic, minced
2 tablespoons snipped fresh parsley
1 teaspoon dried thyme, crushed
1 teaspoon dried marjoram, crushed
¼ teaspoon pepper
4½ cups chicken broth (see tip, page 29)

2½ cups chopped cooked chicken
1 14½-ounce can stewed tomatoes

1 Rinse beans; drain. In a large saucepan combine beans and the 6 cups water. Bring to boiling, reduce heat. Simmer, uncovered, for 2 minutes. Remove from heat. Cover and let stand for 1 hour. (Or, skip the boiling step and soak beans overnight in a covered pan.) Drain and rinse beans.

2 Meanwhile, in a 3½-, 4-, or 5-quart crockery cooker combine onion, fennel, carrots, garlic, parsley, thyme, marjoram, and pepper. Place beans atop vegetables. Pour chicken broth over all.

3 Cover; cook on low-heat setting for 8 to 10 hours or on high-heat setting for 4 to 5 hours.

4 If using low-heat setting, turn to high-heat setting. Stir in chicken and *undrained* tomatoes. Cover and cook for 30 minutes longer or until heated through on high-heat setting. Makes 4 to 6 servings.

Per serving: 471 calories, 44 g protein, 46 g carbohydrate, 13 g total fat (3 g saturated), 74 mg cholesterol, 1,250 mg sodium, 1,304 mg potassium

Tomato and Rice Soup with Pesto

Basil-flavored pesto can be found on the grocery shelf or in the refrigerator section next to the fresh pastas.

1 **cup chopped onion**
1 **cup shredded carrot**
3 **stalks celery with leaves, chopped**
1 **14½-ounce can Italian-style stewed tomatoes**
1 **6-ounce can Italian-style tomato paste**
½ **teaspoon dried oregano, crushed**
¼ **teaspoon dried thyme, crushed**
¼ **teaspoon pepper**
2 **cups water**
2 **cups chicken broth or vegetable broth (see tip page 29)**

1 **cup quick-cooking rice**
¼ **cup pesto**
   Grated Parmesan cheese (optional)

1 In a 3½- or 4-quart crockery cooker combine onion, carrot, celery, *undrained* tomatoes, tomato paste, oregano, thyme, and pepper. Stir in water and chicken or vegetable broth.

2 Cover; cook on low-heat setting for 8 to 10 hours or on high-heat setting for 4 to 5 hours.

3 Stir in rice. Cover; let stand 6 to 7 minutes or till rice is tender. Stir in pesto. Ladle soup into bowls. Sprinkle with grated Parmesan cheese, if desired. Serves 6.

Per serving: 229 calories, 7 g protein, 33 g carbohydrate, 8 g total fat (0 g saturated), 2 mg cholesterol, 876 mg sodium, 725 mg potassium

Sausage Escarole Soup

*Substitute curly endive or another mildly bitter
green for the escarole if you like.*

1 **beaten egg**
2 **tablespoons milk**
¼ **cup fine dry bread crumbs**
1 **pound bulk Italian sausage**
  Nonstick spray coating

2 **15-ounce cans great northern beans,
    drained**
2 **medium carrots, cut into ½-inch pieces**
2 **medium tomatoes, chopped**
½ **cup chopped onion**
2 **cloves garlic, minced**
1 **teaspoon dried Italian seasoning,
    crushed**
½ **teaspoon crushed red pepper**
5 **cups chicken broth (see tip, page 29)**

4 **cups chopped escarole**
  Grated Parmesan cheese

1 For meatballs, in a large bowl combine egg, milk, and bread crumbs. Add sausage and mix well. Shape into 1-inch meatballs. Spray a 12-inch skillet with nonstick coating. Add meatballs and brown on all sides over medium heat. Drain meatballs.

2 In a 3½-, 4-, or 5-quart crockery cooker place beans, carrots, tomatoes, onion, garlic, Italian seasoning, and red pepper. Add meatballs to cooker. Pour broth over all.

3 Cover; cook on low-heat setting for 8 to 10 hours or on high-heat setting for 4 to 5 hours. Stir in escarole. Ladle into bowls. Sprinkle with grated Parmesan cheese. Makes 6 servings.

Per serving: 383 calories, 28 g protein, 32 g carbohydrate, 19 g total fat (7 g saturated), 83 mg cholesterol, 1,531 mg sodium, 924 mg potassium

Calico Ham and Bean Soup

Try a pound of purchased bean mix or a pound of any one of the beans for this soup. For thicker soup, mash part of the beans before serving.

½ **cup dry navy or great northern beans**
½ **cup dry black beans or kidney beans**
½ **cup dry lima beans**
½ **cup dry garbanzo beans**
½ **cup dry split peas**
6 **cups water**

2 **cups fully cooked ham cut into**
     ½-inch pieces (about 10 ounces)
1 **cup chopped onion**
1 **cup chopped carrot**
1 **teaspoon dried basil, crushed**
1 **teaspoon dried oregano, crushed**
¾ **teaspoon salt**
¼ **teaspoon pepper**
2 **bay leaves**
6 **cups water**

  Salt
  Pepper

1 Rinse beans: drain. In a large saucepan combine the beans, peas, and the 6 cups water. Bring to boiling; reduce heat. Simmer, uncovered, for 10 minutes. Drain and rinse beans.

2 Meanwhile, in a 3½-, 4-, or 5-quart crockery cooker combine ham, onion, carrot, basil, oregano, ¾ teaspoon salt, ¼ teaspoon pepper, and bay leaves. Stir in drained beans and the remaining 6 cups fresh water.

3 Cover; cook on low-heat setting for 8 to 10 hours or on high-heat setting for 4 to 5 hours. Discard the bay leaves. Season to taste with additional salt and pepper. Makes 8 servings.

Per serving: *244 calories, 19 g protein, 36 g carbohydrate, 3 g total fat (1 g saturated), 11 mg cholesterol, 696 mg sodium, 704 mg potassium*

Beef and Spinach Soup with Rice

Make this into a lamb soup by substituting lamb stew
meat for the beef and replacing the thyme and basil with ¾ teaspoon
dried rosemary and ¼ teaspoon dried mint.

1½ **pounds beef stew meat, cut into**
    1-inch cubes
1 **tablespoon cooking oil**

2 **medium carrots, cut into ½-inch**
    slices (1 cup)
2 **medium yellow summer squash,**
    halved lengthwise, and cut into
    ½-inch slices (2½ cups)
1 **cup chopped onion**
1 **clove garlic, minced**
¾ **teaspoon dried thyme, crushed**
¾ **teaspoon dried basil, crushed**
6 **cups beef broth (see tip, page 29)**
¼ **cup dry red or white wine (optional)**

2 **cups chopped fresh spinach**
½ **cup quick-cooking rice**

1 Trim off fat from meat. In a large skillet brown meat, *half* at a time, in hot oil. Drain off the fat.

2 In a 3½- 4-, or 5-quart crockery cooker place carrots, squash, onion, garlic, thyme, and basil. Place meat atop vegetables. Pour broth and wine (if desired), over all.

3 Cover; cook on low-heat setting for 8 to 10 hours or on high-heat setting for 4 to 5 hours.

4 Stir in spinach and rice. Cover and let stand 5 to 10 minutes or till rice is tender. Makes 8 servings.

Per serving: 213 calories, 25 g protein, 11 g carbohydrate, 8 g total fat (3 g saturated), 62 mg cholesterol, 693 mg sodium, 604 mg potassium

Hearty Beef Stew

Purchase stew meat, already cut, from the butcher. Or, purchase a beef chuck,
or shoulder, roast and cut into 1- to 1½-inch pieces.

1 **pound beef stew meat**
1 **tablespoon cooking oil**

12 **ounces small red potatoes, quartered**
   (about 2 cups)
4 **medium carrots, cut into ½-inch**
   pieces (2 cups)

1 **10¾-ounce can condensed cream of**
   mushroom or cream of celery soup
½ **cup dry red wine or beef broth (if**
   using beef broth see tip, page 29)
1 **envelope regular onion soup mix**
½ **teaspoon dried marjoram or thyme,**
   crushed (optional)
1 **9-ounce package frozen cut green**
   beans, thawed

1 In a large skillet brown meat, *half* at a time, in hot oil. Drain off fat.

2 In a 3½- or 4-quart crockery cooker place potatoes, carrots, and meat.

3 In a bowl combine condensed soup, wine or broth, soup mix, and marjoram or thyme, if desired. Pour over meat.

4 Cover; cook on low-heat setting for 8 to 10 hours or on high-heat setting for 4 to 5 hours. Stir in thawed green beans. Cook for an additional 5 to 10 minutes longer. Makes 4 servings.

Per serving: 489 calories, 32 g protein, 41 g carbohydrate, 20 g total fat (6 g saturated), 77 mg cholesterol, 1,625 mg sodium, 1,092 mg potassium

Beef Stew

The long, slow cooking of the crockery cooker will make the beef or pork fork-tender. Serve with biscuits and a mixed green salad.

2 tablespoons all-purpose flour
1 pound beef or pork stew meat, cut into
   1-inch cubes
2 tablespoons cooking oil

2¼ cups cubed, peeled potatoes
2 cups sliced carrots
1 cup sliced celery
½ cup chopped onion
2 teaspoons instant beef
   bouillon granules
2 cloves garlic, minced
1 teaspoon dried basil, crushed
½ teaspoon dried thyme, crushed
2½ cups vegetable juice

1 Place flour in a plastic bag. Add meat cubes, a few at a time, shaking to coat meat with flour. In a large skillet brown meat, *half* at a time, in hot oil. Drain off fat.

2 Meanwhile, in the bottom of a 3½- or 4-quart crockery cooker layer potatoes, carrots, celery, and onion. Sprinkle with bouillon granules, garlic, basil, and thyme; add meat. Pour vegetable juice over meat.

3 Cover; cook on low-heat setting for 7 to 8 hours or on high-heat setting for 3½ to 4½ hours or till meat and vegetables are tender. Makes 4 servings.

Per serving: *369 calories, 31 g protein, 34 g carbohydrate, 12 g total fat (4 g saturated), 82 mg cholesterol, 1,096 mg sodium, 1,003 mg potassium*

Spiced Beef and Jerusalem Artichoke Stew

Look for Jerusalem artichokes, also called sunchokes,
in your produce department, fall through winter. These tubers taste
similar to an artichoke when cooked.

1 **pound boneless beef chuck steak,**
   cut into ¾-inch cubes
1 **tablespoon olive oil or cooking oil**

8 **whole allspice**
½ **teaspoon dillseed**
1 **bay leaf**

1 **14½-ounce can tomatoes, cut up**
1 **8-ounce can tomato sauce**
2 **tablespoons cider vinegar**
2 **cloves garlic, minced**
¼ **teaspoon celery salt**
¼ **teaspoon pepper**

1 **pound Jerusalem artichokes, cut into**
   ¼-inch thick slices
2 **cups frozen pearl onions or 1 medium**
   onion, cut into thin wedges
8 **ounces fresh mushrooms, halved**

1 In a large skillet brown meat, *half* at a time, in hot oil. Drain off fat.

2 For spice bag, place allspice, dillseed, and bay leaf in the center of a square of 100 percent cotton cheesecloth. Bring up the corners and tie them with a clean string. Set aside.

3 In a bowl stir together *undrained* tomatoes, tomato sauce, vinegar, garlic, celery salt, and pepper.

4 In a 3½- or 4-quart crockery cooker place Jerusalem artichokes, onions, and mushrooms. Add meat and spice bag. Pour tomato mixture over all.

5 Cover; cook on low-heat setting for 9 to 10 hours or on high-heat setting for 4 to 5 hours. Remove and discard spice bag before serving. Makes 5 servings.

Per serving: 313 calories, 27 g protein, 34 g carbohydrate, 9 g total fat (3 g saturated), 66 mg cholesterol, 546 mg sodium, 1,241 mg potassium

Borscht Stew

*When peeling fresh beets, wear rubber gloves to
protect your hands from stains.*

1   **pound boneless beef bottom round
    steak, cut into 1-inch pieces**
1   **tablespoon cooking oil**

4   **medium beets, peeled and cut into
    ½-inch pieces or one 16-ounce can
    diced beets, drained**
2   **medium tomatoes, coarsely chopped**
2   **medium potatoes, peeled and cut into
    ½-inch pieces**
2   **medium carrots, shredded**
1   **medium onion, chopped**
3   **cloves garlic, minced**

4   **cups beef broth (see tip, page 29)**
1   **6-ounce can tomato paste**
2   **tablespoons red wine vinegar**
1   **tablespoon brown sugar**
1   **tablespoon snipped fresh parsley**
1   **teaspoon salt**
½   **teaspoon dried dillweed**
¼   **teaspoon pepper**
1   **bay leaf**

3   **cups shredded cabbage
    Dairy sour cream or plain yogurt**

1   In a large skillet brown beef, *half* at a
time, in hot oil. Drain off fat.

2   Meanwhile, in a 3½-, 4-, or 5-quart crockery cooker combine beets, tomatoes, potatoes, carrots, onion, and garlic. Add meat.

3   In a bowl combine beef broth, tomato
paste, vinegar, brown sugar, parsley, salt, dillweed, pepper, and bay leaf. Add to cooker.

4   Cover; cook on low-heat setting for 7½ to
9½ hours or on high-heat setting for 3½ to
4½ hours.

5   If using low-heat setting, turn to high-heat
setting. Stir in cabbage. Cover and cook
30 minutes longer on high-heat setting. Discard bay leaf. Ladle into bowls. Garnish
each serving with a dollop of sour cream or
yogurt. Makes 6 servings.

*Per serving: 299 calories, 24 g protein, 31 g carbohy-
drate, 10 g total fat (4 g saturated), 54 mg cholesterol,
990 mg sodium, 1,228 mg potassium*

Pork and Hominy Stew

Pork, hominy, and chili powder are combined to make a flavorful rendition of pozole. Hominy, dried corn that has had the hulls removed, is found in the canned vegetable section of the supermarket.

1 **pound boneless pork shoulder**
1 **tablespoon cooking oil**

1 **medium red or green sweet pepper, cut into ½-inch pieces**
1 **medium tomato, chopped**
½ **cup chopped onion**
4 **cloves garlic, minced**
2 **16-ounce cans golden hominy, drained**
1 **4-ounce can diced green chili peppers, drained**
1 **tablespoon chili powder**
½ **teaspoon dried oregano, crushed**
2 **14½-ounce cans chicken broth (see tip, page 29)**

Tortilla chips (optional)

1 Trim fat from meat; cut pork into 1-inch cubes. In a large skillet brown pork, *half* at a time, in hot oil. Drain off fat.

2 Transfer pork to a 3½-, 4-, or 5-quart crockery cooker. Add sweet pepper, tomato, onion, garlic, hominy, chili peppers, chili powder, and oregano. Pour broth over all.

3 Cover; cook on low-heat setting for 8 to 10 hours or on high-heat setting for 4 to 5 hours. Serve with tortilla chips, if desired. Makes 6 servings.

Per serving: 289 calories, 19 g protein, 27 g carbohydrate, 11 g total fat (3 g saturated), 50 mg cholesterol, 897 mg sodium, 457 mg potassium

Spicy Southwestern Beef Stew

If jalapeño pinto beans are not available in your area,
add one finely chopped jalapeño pepper.

1 pound beef chuck pot roast
1 tablespoon cooking oil

2 14½-ounce cans Mexican-style stewed
    tomatoes
1½ cups coarsely chopped onion
1 15-ounce can pinto beans or jalapeño
    pinto beans

3½ cups beef broth (see tip, page 29)
1 6-ounce can tomato paste
4 teaspoons chili powder
1 tablespoon dried Italian
    seasoning, crushed
½ teaspoon crushed red pepper
¼ teaspoon ground cloves
¼ teaspoon ground allspice
¼ teaspoon ground cinnamon
1 medium zucchini, halved lengthwise,
    and cut into ½-inch pieces
1 medium yellow or green sweet
    pepper, cut into 1-inch pieces

1 Trim fat from meat. Cut meat into 1-inch cubes. In a large skillet brown meat, *half* at a time, in hot oil. Drain off fat.

2 Transfer meat to a 3½-, 4-, or 5-quart crockery cooker. Add *undrained* tomatoes, onion, and beans.

3 In a bowl combine beef broth, tomato paste, chili powder, Italian seasoning, crushed red pepper, cloves, allspice, and cinnamon. Add to cooker.

4 Cover; cook on low-heat setting for 10 to 12 hours or on high-heat setting for 5 to 6 hours.

5 If using low-heat setting, turn to high-heat setting. Add zucchini and sweet peppers. Cover and cook 30 minutes longer on high-heat setting. Makes 6 servings.

Per serving: 360 calories, 35 g protein, 35 g carbohydrate, 10 g total fat (3 g saturated), 76 mg cholesterol, 1,258 mg sodium, 1,253 mg potassium

Tex-Mex Chili

*For more hotness, add one or two chopped jalapeño peppers and use hot-style
tomato juice cocktail. Serve with crushed red pepper.*

1 **pound ground beef or bulk pork
  sausage**
2 **cloves garlic, minced**
3 **to 4 teaspoons chili powder**
½ **teaspoon ground cumin**

1 **15½-ounce can red kidney
  beans, drained**
1 **cup chopped celery**
1 **cup chopped onion**
½ **cup chopped green sweet pepper**
1 **16-ounce can tomatoes, cut up**
1 **10-ounce can tomatoes with green
  chili peppers**
1 **cup vegetable juice or tomato juice**
1 **6-ounce can tomato paste**
¼ **teaspoon salt**

Shredded cheddar cheese
Dairy sour cream

1 In a large skillet cook the beef or sausage
and garlic till meat is brown. Drain off fat.
Stir in chili powder and cumin; cook 2 minutes more.

2 Meanwhile, in a 3½-, 4-, or 5-quart crockery cooker combine beans, celery, onion,
and green sweet pepper. Add *undrained*
tomatoes, *undrained* tomatoes with chili peppers, vegetable juice or tomato juice, tomato
paste, and salt. Stir in meat mixture.

3 Cover; cook on low-heat setting for 8 to
10 hours or on high-heat setting for 4 to 5
hours. Ladle chili into soup bowls. Pass
shredded cheese and sour cream with chili.
Makes 4 to 6 servings.

*Per serving: 482 calories, 36 g protein, 46 g carbohy-
drate, 21 g total fat (9 g saturated), 85 mg cholesterol,
1,263 mg sodium, 1,584 mg potassium*

White Chili

*For the cooked chicken, poach three or four skinned and boned
chicken breast halves in boiling water or chicken broth, covered, for about 12
minutes or until no pink remains. Drain, cool slightly, then chop.*

3   15-ounce cans great northern, pinto,
      or cannellini beans, drained
2½ cups chopped cooked chicken
1   cup chopped onion
1½ cups chopped red, green, and/or
      yellow sweet pepper
2   jalapeño chili peppers, stemmed and
      chopped
2   cloves garlic, minced
2   teaspoons ground cumin
½   teaspoon salt
½   teaspoon dried oregano, crushed
3½ cups chicken broth (see tip, page 29)

    Shredded Monterey Jack cheese
      (optional)
    Broken tortilla chips (optional)

1 In a 3½-, 4-, or 5-quart crockery cooker
combine the drained beans, chicken,
onion, sweet pepper, jalapeño peppers,
garlic, cumin, salt, and oregano. Stir in
chicken broth.

2 Cover; cook on low-heat setting for 8
to 10 hours or high-heat setting for 4 to
5 hours.

3 Ladle the soup into bowls. Top each
serving with some cheese and tortilla chips,
if desired. Makes 8 servings.

*Per serving: 310 calories, 28 g protein, 38 g carbohy-
drate, 5 g total fat (1 g saturated), 43 mg cholesterol,
523 mg sodium, 862 mg potassium*

Chunky Vegetable Clam Chowder

Warm up a chilly fall day with this hearty soup—satisfying enough even for the most ravenous appetite.

2 6½-ounce cans minced clams

2 cups peeled potatoes, cut into
      ½-inch cubes
1 cup finely chopped onion
1 cup chopped celery
½ cup shredded carrot
1 teaspoon sugar
¼ teaspoon salt
¼ teaspoon pepper
2 10¾-ounce cans condensed cream
      of potato soup
2 cups water

1 cup nonfat dry milk powder
⅓ cup all-purpose flour
1 cup cold water

4 slices bacon, crisp-cooked, drained,
      and crumbled
   Paprika

1 Drain clams, reserving liquid. Cover clams; chill.

2 In a 3½-, 4-, or 5-quart crockery cooker combine reserved clam liquid, potatoes, onion, celery, carrot, sugar, salt, and pepper. Stir in potato soup and 2 cups water.

3 Cover; cook on low-heat setting for 8 to 10 hours or on high-heat setting for 4 to 5 hours.

4 If using low-heat setting, turn to high-heat setting. In a medium bowl combine nonfat dry milk powder and flour. Gradually whisk in 1 cup cold water; stir into soup. Cover; cook on high-heat setting 10 to 15 minutes or till thickened.

5 Stir in clams. Cover; cook 5 minutes more. Ladle soup into bowls. Sprinkle each serving with crumbled bacon and paprika. Makes 6 to 8 servings.

Per serving: 268 calories, 14 g protein, 43 g carbohydrate, 5 g total fat (2 g saturated), 49 mg cholesterol, 735 mg sodium, 841 mg potassium

Brunswick Fish Chowder

Adding the fish partially frozen keeps it from overcooking.
And, if you're watching your sodium-intake, try sodium-reduced soups
and broths available at your grocery store.

1 **pound frozen cod or whiting fillets**

2 **medium potatoes, finely chopped**
1 **cup chopped onion**
2 **cloves garlic, minced**
1 **10¾-ounce can condensed cream of**
   celery soup
1 **10-ounce package frozen whole**
   kernel corn
1 **10-ounce package frozen baby**
   lima beans
1½ **cups chicken broth (see tip, page 29)**
⅓ **cup dry white wine or water**
1 **teaspoon lemon-pepper seasoning**
1 **bay leaf**

1 **14½-ounce can stewed tomatoes**
⅓ **cup nonfat dry milk powder**

1 Let fish stand at room temperature while preparing other ingredients.

2 In a 3½-, 4-, or 5-quart crockery cooker combine potatoes, onion, garlic, soup, frozen corn, frozen lima beans, chicken broth, white wine or water, lemon-pepper seasoning, and bay leaf. Halve the fillets crosswise; place frozen fish fillet halves in the cooker.

3 Cover; cook on low-heat setting for 7 to 8 hours or on high-heat setting for 3½ to 4 hours.

4 Discard bay leaf. Break fish into bite-size chunks with a fork. Stir in *undrained* tomatoes and dry milk powder. Makes 6 servings.

Per serving: *300 calories, 23 g protein, 44 g carbohydrate, 4 g total fat (1 g saturated), 37 mg cholesterol, 1,058 mg sodium, 1,012 mg potassium*

Manhattan Clam Chowder

To save time and retain the nutrients, don't peel the potatoes.
Just scrub them, then cut into cubes.

2 6½-ounce cans minced clams

2 cups peeled potatoes, cut into
    ½-inch cubes
1 cup chopped onion
1 cup chopped celery with leaves
½ cup chopped green sweet pepper
1 14½-ounce can Italian-style
    stewed tomatoes
1½ cups hot-style tomato juice or hot-style
    vegetable juice
½ teaspoon salt
½ teaspoon dried thyme, crushed
1 bay leaf

4 slices bacon, crisp-cooked, drained,
    and crumbled

1 Drain clams, reserving liquid. Cover clams; chill.

2 In a 3½- or 4-quart crockery cooker combine reserved clam liquid, potatoes, onion, celery, green sweet pepper, *undrained* tomatoes, tomato juice or vegetable juice, salt, thyme, and bay leaf.

3 Cover; cook on low-heat setting for 8 to 10 hours or on high-heat setting for 4 to 5 hours.

4 If using low-heat setting, turn to high-heat setting. Stir in clams. Cover and cook on high-heat setting 5 minutes. Discard bay leaf. Ladle soup into bowls. Sprinkle each serving with crumbled bacon. Serves 6.

Per serving: 146 calories, 9 g protein, 24 g carbohydrate, 3 g total fat (1 g saturated), 42 mg cholesterol, 761 mg sodium, 751 mg potassium

Easy Cassoulet

A streamlined, healthful version of the classic French dish.

8 ounces skinless, boneless chicken
    thighs

2 medium carrots, cut into ½-inch pieces
1 medium red or green sweet pepper, cut
    into ½-inch pieces
1 cup chopped onion
3 cloves garlic, minced
2 15-ounce cans cannellini beans or great
    northern beans, rinsed and drained
1 14½-ounce can Italian-style
    stewed tomatoes
8 ounces fully cooked smoked turkey
    sausage, halved lengthwise and cut
    into ½-inch slices

1½ cups chicken broth (see tip, page 29)
½ cup dry white wine or chicken broth
1 tablespoon snipped fresh parsley
1 teaspoon dried thyme, crushed
¼ teaspoon ground red pepper
1 bay leaf

1 Rinse chicken; pat dry. Cut chicken into 1-inch pieces.

2 In a 3½-, 4-, or 5-quart crockery cooker place carrots, sweet pepper, onion, garlic, beans, *undrained* tomatoes, chicken, and sausage.

3 In a bowl combine chicken broth, wine, parsley, thyme, red pepper, and bay leaf. Add to cooker.

4 Cover; cook on low-heat setting for 7 to 8 hours or on high-heat setting for 3½ to 4 hours. Discard bay leaf. Makes 6 servings.

Per serving: 259 calories, 22 g protein, 31 g carbohydrate, 7 g total fat (2 g saturated), 44 mg cholesterol, 974 mg sodium, 726 mg potassium

Chicken and Sausage Gumbo

To ease a last minute time crunch, make the roux ahead of time. When cooked,
the roux should be a coppery color, similar to a tarnished penny.

⅓ **cup all-purpose flour**
⅓ **cup cooking oil**

3 **cups water**
12 **ounces fully cooked smoked sausage**
links, quartered and sliced
lengthwise
1½ **cups chopped cooked chicken or**
12-ounces skinless, boneless
chicken breasts or thighs, cut into
¾-inch pieces
2 **cups sliced okra or one 10-ounce**
package frozen whole okra,
partially thawed and cut into
½-inch slices
1 **cup chopped onion**
½ **cup chopped green sweet pepper**
½ **cup chopped celery**
4 **cloves garlic, minced**
½ **teaspoon salt**
½ **teaspoon pepper**
¼ **teaspoon ground red pepper**

3 **cups hot cooked rice**

1 For the roux, in a heavy 2-quart saucepan stir together the flour and oil till smooth. Cook over medium-high heat for 5 minutes, stirring constantly. Reduce heat to medium. Cook and stir constantly about 15 minutes more or till a dark, reddish-brown roux forms. Cool.

2 In a 3½-, 4-, or 5-quart crockery cooker place water. Stir in roux. Add sausage, chicken, okra, onion, sweet pepper, celery, garlic, salt, pepper, and ground red pepper.

3 Cover; cook on low-heat setting for 6 to 7 hours or on high-heat setting for 3 to 3½ hours. Skim off fat. Serve over the hot cooked rice. Makes 5 servings.

Per serving: 637 calories, 28 g protein, 45 g carbohydrate, 39 g total fat (11 g saturated), 83 mg cholesterol, 952 mg sodium, 571 mg potassium

Chicken and Sausage Cassoulet

An easy, delicious version of the classic French dish
called cassoulet. Traditionally, it is made with beans and various meats.
The exact combinations of ingredients varies by regions.

3 **medium carrots, cut into ½-inch**
    pieces (1 cup)
1 **medium onion, chopped (½ cup)**
⅓ **cup water**

1 **6-ounce can tomato paste**
½ **cup dry red wine or water**
1 **teaspoon garlic powder**
½ **teaspoon dried thyme, crushed**
⅛ **teaspoon ground cloves**
2 **bay leaves**
2 **15-ounce cans navy beans, drained**
4 **skinless, boneless chicken breast halves**
8 **ounces fully cooked Polish sausage,**
    cut into ¼-inch slices

1 In a small saucepan combine the carrots, onion, and ⅓ cup water. Bring to boiling; reduce heat. Simmer, covered, for 8 minutes. Transfer the mixture to a 3½- or 4-quart crockery cooker.

2 Stir in tomato paste, wine or water, garlic powder, thyme, cloves, and bay leaves. Add beans. Place chicken atop bean mixture. Place sausage atop chicken.

3 Cover; cook on low-heat setting for 5 to 7 hours or on high-heat setting for 2½ to 3½ hours. Before serving, discard bay leaves and skim off fat. Makes 4 servings.

Per serving: 657 calories, 49 g protein, 64 g carbohydrate, 21 g total fat (7 g saturated), 99 mg cholesterol, 1,659 mg sodium, 1,563 mg potassium

Meats

Beef Pot Roast

Piping hot yeast rolls are a perfect accompaniment.

1   2- to 2½-pound boneless beef chuck
        pot roast
1   tablespoon cooking oil

1   pound whole tiny new potatoes,
        3 medium potatoes, or 3 medium
        sweet potatoes
8   carrots or parsnips, cut into
        1-inch pieces
3   small onions, cut into wedges

¾   cup water, dry red or white wine, or
        tomato juice
1   tablespoon Worcestershire sauce
2   teaspoons instant beef
        bouillon granules
1   teaspoon dried basil, crushed

½   cup cold water
¼   cup all-purpose flour

1   Trim fat from pot roast. If necessary, cut roast to fit into crockery cooker. In a large skillet brown roast on all sides in hot oil.

2   Meanwhile, remove a narrow strip of peel from the center of each new potato, or peel and quarter each medium potato. In a 3½- or 4-quart crockery cooker place potatoes, carrots or parsnips, and onions. Place meat atop vegetables.

3   In a small bowl combine ¾ cup water, wine, or tomato juice; Worcestershire sauce; bouillon granules; and basil. Pour over meat and vegetables.

4   Cover; cook on low-heat setting for 10 to 12 hours or on high-heat setting for 5 to 6 hours.

5   Remove meat and vegetables from cooker and place on platter; keep warm. Pour juices into glass measuring cup. Skim fat. If necessary, add water to equal 1½ cups juice. Transfer to saucepan. Combine the ½ cup cold water and flour; stir into the juices in saucepan. Cook and stir till thickened and bubbly. Cook and stir 1 minute more. Season to taste with salt and pepper. Makes 6 to 8 servings.

Per serving: 505 calories, 54 g protein, 32 g carbohydrate, 17 g total fat (6 g saturated), 153 mg cholesterol, 466 mg sodium, 1,016 mg potassium

Pot Roast with Herbed-Port Gravy

*A wonderfully seasoned gravy that would
also be tasty over mashed potatoes. If you don't have port or
marsala on hand, substitute a dry red wine.*

1 2½- to 3-pound beef chuck pot roast
1 tablespoon cooking oil

½ cup chopped onion
½ cup port or marsala
¼ cup catsup
3 tablespoons quick-cooking tapioca
1 tablespoon Worcestershire sauce
1 teaspoon dried thyme, crushed
1 teaspoon dried oregano, crushed
2 cloves garlic, minced

4 cups hot cooked noodles

1 Trim fat from pot roast. If necessary, cut roast to fit into crockery cooker. In a large skillet brown roast on all sides in hot oil. Drain off fat. Transfer the meat to a 3½- or 4-quart crockery cooker.

2 In a bowl combine onion, port or marsala, catsup, tapioca, Worcestershire, thyme, oregano, and garlic. Pour over pot roast.

3 Cover; cook on low-heat setting for 8 to 10 hours or on high-heat setting for 4 to 5 hours. Transfer roast to a serving platter. Skim fat from gravy. Pass gravy with meat. Serve with hot cooked noodles. Makes 8 to 10 servings.

Per serving: 377 calories, 35 g protein, 29 g carbohydrate, 11 g total fat (4 g saturated), 119 mg cholesterol, 187 mg sodium, 378 mg potassium

Pot Roast with Noodles

Old-fashioned goodness that will have your family asking for seconds.

1 2- to 2½-pound beef chuck pot roast
1 tablespoon cooking oil

2 medium carrots, coarsely chopped
2 stalks celery, sliced
1 medium onion, sliced
2 cloves garlic, minced
1 tablespoon quick-cooking tapioca

1 14½-ounce can Italian-style
     stewed tomatoes
1 6-ounce can Italian-style tomato paste
1 tablespoon brown sugar
½ teaspoon salt
¼ teaspoon pepper
1 bay leaf

4 cups hot cooked noodles

1 Trim fat from pot roast. If necessary, cut roast to fit into crockery cooker. In a large skillet brown roast on all sides in hot oil.

2 Meanwhile, in a 3½- or 4-quart crockery cooker place carrots, celery, onion, and garlic. Sprinkle tapioca over vegetables. Place meat atop vegetables.

3 In a bowl combine *undrained* tomatoes, tomato paste, brown sugar, salt, pepper, and bay leaf; pour over the meat.

4 Cover; cook on low-heat setting for 10 to 12 hours or on high-heat setting for 4 to 5 hours. Discard bay leaf. Skim off fat. Serve with hot cooked noodles. Makes 8 servings.

Per serving: 409 calories, 38 g protein, 34 g carbohydrate, 12 g total fat (4 g saturated), 127 mg cholesterol, 607 mg sodium, 744 mg potassium

Harvest Dinner

This old-fashioned dinner favorite is seasoned with a touch of cinnamon.
If you prefer, skip the gravy and spoon the juices over the meat.

1   **1½- to 2-pound boneless beef chuck**
    pot roast
1   **tablespoon cooking oil**

1   **medium onion, sliced**
4   **medium sweet potatoes, peeled and**
    quartered (1¼ pounds)

¾   **cup water**
1½ **teaspoons instant beef bouillon**
    granules
¼   **teaspoon celery seed**
¼   **teaspoon ground cinnamon**
¼   **teaspoon pepper**

2   **tablespoons cornstarch**
2   **tablespoons cold water**
    Apple wedges (optional)

1   Trim the fat from the pot roast. In a large skillet brown roast on all sides in hot oil. Drain well.

2   In a 3½- or 4-quart crockery cooker place the onion, then the sweet potatoes. Place meat atop vegetables. (Cut roast, if necessary to fit.)

3   In a small bowl combine water, bouillon granules, celery seed, cinnamon, and pepper. Pour over meat and vegetables.

4   Cover; cook on low-heat setting for 8 to 10 hours or on high-heat setting for 4 to 5 hours.

5   Remove meat and vegetables from cooker and place on platter; reserve juices. Skim fat from juices. Pass juices. Or, for gravy, pour juices into glass measuring cup. If necessary, add water to equal 2 cups juice. In a saucepan stir cornstarch into 2 tablespoons cold water; add juices. Cook and stir till thickened and bubbly. Cook and stir 2 minutes more. Serve gravy with roast and vegetables. Garnish platter with apple wedges, if desired. Makes 6 servings.

Per serving: 328 calories, 30 g protein, 30 g carbohydrate, 10 g total fat (3 g saturated), 82 mg cholesterol, 282 mg sodium, 655 mg potassium

Herbed Mushroom Round Steak

*Bottom roound steak, less expensive than top
round steak, is a good choice for the cockery cooker as the moist-heat
cooking tenderizes the meat.*

2 pounds beef round steak, cut ¾ inch thick
1 tablespoon cooking oil

1 medium onion, sliced
2 cups sliced fresh mushrooms or two 4-ounce jars canned mushrooms

1 10¾-ounce can condensed cream of mushroom soup
¼ cup dry white wine (optional)
½ teaspoon dried oregano, crushed
¼ teaspoon dried thyme, crushed
¼ teaspoon pepper

3 cups hot cooked noodles

1 Trim fat from meat. Cut meat into serving-size portions. In a large skillet brown beef on both sides in hot oil.

2 In a 3½- or 4-quart crockery cooker place onion slices and mushrooms. Place beef on top of vegetables.

3 In a small bowl combine soup, wine (if desired), oregano, thyme, and pepper; pour over meat.

4 Cover; cook on low-heat setting for 8 to 10 hours or on high-heat setting for 4 to 5 hours. Serve over hot cooked noodles. Makes 6 servings.

Per serving: *414 calories, 42 g protein, 27 g carbohydrate, 15 g total fat (4 g saturated), 123 mg cholesterol, 488 mg sodium, 688 mg potassium*

Beef and Vegetables in Red Wine Sauce

*Serve this company fare with fresh noodles found in the
refrigerated section of your supermarket.*

1½ **pounds boneless beef bottom round
steak, cut into 1-inch cubes**
1 **tablespoon cooking oil**

2 **medium carrots, cut into ½-inch pieces**
2 **stalks celery, cut into ½-inch pieces**
1 **cup quartered fresh mushrooms**
½ **cup sliced green onions**
3 **tablespoons quick-cooking tapioca**

1 **14½-ounce can Italian-style stewed
tomatoes**
1 **cup beef broth (see tip, page 29)**
½ **cup dry red wine, white wine, or
beef broth**
1 **teaspoon dried Italian
seasoning, crushed**
½ **teaspoon salt**
¼ **teaspoon pepper**
1 **bay leaf**

3 **cups hot cooked noodles**

1 Trim fat from meat; cut into 1-inch cubes.
In a large skillet brown beef, *half* at a time,
in hot oil. Drain off fat.

2 Transfer beef to a 3½- or 4-quart crockery
cooker. Add carrots, celery, mushrooms, and
green onions. Sprinkle with tapioca.

3 Combine *undrained* tomatoes, beef broth,
wine or broth, Italian seasoning, salt, pepper, and bay leaf. Pour over vegetables and
meat.

4 Cover; cook on low-heat setting for 8
to 10 hours or on high-heat setting for 4 to
5 hours. Discard bay leaf. Serve over hot
cooked noodles. Makes 6 to 8 servings.

*Per serving: 365 calories, 33 g protein, 34 g carbohy-
drate, 9 g total fat (3 g saturated), 98 mg cholesterol,
662 mg sodium, 847 mg potassium*

Spiced Beef Brisket

*For a real time-saver, freeze half of this plentiful main course. It'll be
ready in minutes for dinner on a busy day.*

1 **3½- to 4-pound fresh beef brisket**

2 **cups water**
¼ **cup catsup**
1 **envelope regular onion soup mix**
2 **tablespoons Worcestershire sauce**
½ **teaspoon ground cinnamon**
½ **teaspoon bottled minced garlic**
¼ **teaspoon pepper**

¼ **cup cold water**
4 **teaspoons all-purpose flour**

1 Place beef in a 3½- to 4-quart crockery cooker. If necessary, cut brisket to fit into the cooker.

2 In a mixing bowl combine the 2 cups water, catsup, soup mix, Worcestershire sauce, cinnamon, garlic, and pepper. Pour over brisket.

3 Cover; cook on a low-heat setting for 8 to 10 hours.

4 Remove beef; keep warm. Pour juices into a glass measuring cup. Skim fat. Transfer ¾ *cup* of the liquid to a moisture- and vapor-proof container. Cool slightly. Seal, label, and freeze up to 6 months. For gravy, in a small saucepan stir the ¼ cup cold water into the flour. Stir in another ¼ *cup* cooking liquid. Cook and stir till thickened and bubbly. Cook and stir 1 minute more.

5 Slice beef thinly across the grain. Transfer *half* of the beef to a moisture- and vapor-proof container. Seal, label, and freeze up to 6 months. Serve remaining beef with the hot gravy. Makes 2 meals (5 or 6 servings each).

Note: To serve frozen meat portion, thaw meat and cooking liquid. Warm meat in a covered baking dish in a 350° oven for 20 minutes. For gravy, in a small saucepan stir together the ¾ cup *cooking liquid*, ¼ cup *cold water*, and 4 teaspoons *all-purpose flour*. Cook and stir till thickened and bubbly. Cook and stir 1 minute more.

Per serving: 310 calories, 35 g protein, 6 g carbohydrate, 15 g total fat (5 g saturated), 110 mg cholesterol, 575 mg sodium, 427 mg potassium

Beef Brisket with Smoky Barbecue Sauce

*You may want to serve this smoke-flavored beef on buns or rolls. Complete the
meal with baked beans, coleslaw, and a dessert.*

1 **2- to 3-pound fresh beef brisket**

1 **teaspoon chili powder**
½ **teaspoon garlic powder**
¼ **teaspoon celery seed**
⅛ **teaspoon pepper**

½ **cup catsup**
½ **cup chili sauce**
¼ **cup packed brown sugar**
2 **tablespoons vinegar**
2 **tablespoons Worcestershire sauce**
1½ **teaspoons liquid smoke**
½ **teaspoon dry mustard**

1 Trim fat from brisket. If necessary, cut
brisket to fit into crockery cooker.

2 Combine chili powder, garlic powder, celery seed, and pepper; rub evenly over meat.
Place meat in a 3½-, 4-, or 5-quart crockery
cooker.

3 For sauce, combine catsup, chili sauce,
brown sugar, vinegar, Worcestershire sauce,
liquid smoke, and dry mustard. Pour over
brisket.

4 Cover; cook on low-heat setting for 8 to
10 hours or on high-heat setting for 4 to 5
hours. Remove meat from cooker. Cut the
brisket into thin slices across the grain.
Skim fat off juices in cooker; serve juices
with meat. Makes 6 to 8 servings.

*Per serving: 358 calories, 34 g protein, 22 g carbohy-
drate, 15 g total fat (5 g saturated), 104 mg cholesterol, 676 mg sodium, 596 mg potassium*

South-of-the-Border Beef Fajitas

*Because chili peppers contain volatile oils that can burn skin
and eyes, avoid direct contact with them. Wear plastic or rubber gloves, or
work under cold running water. If your bare hands touch the chili peppers,
wash your hands and nails well with soap and water.*

1½ **pounds beef flank steak**
1 **cup chopped onion**
1 **green sweet pepper, cut into**
    ½-inch pieces
1 **or 2 jalapeño peppers,chopped**
1 **tablespoon snipped fresh cilantro**
2 **cloves garlic, minced**
1 **teaspoon chili powder**
1 **teaspoon ground cumin**
1 **teaspoon ground coriander**
¼ **teaspoon salt**
1 **8-ounce can stewed tomatoes**

12 **7-inch flour tortillas**
2 **to 3 teaspoons lime juice (optional)**
  Shredded Cojack cheese (optional)
  Guacamole (optional)
  Dairy sour cream (optional)
  Salsa (optional)

1 Trim fat from meat. Cut flank steak into 6 portions. In a 3½-quart crockery cooker combine meat, onion, green sweet pepper, jalapeño pepper(s), cilantro, garlic, chili powder, cumin, coriander, and salt. Add *undrained* tomatoes.

2 Cover; cook on low-heat setting for 8 to 10 hours or on high-heat setting for 4 to 5 hours.

3 To heat tortillas wrap them in foil and heat in a 350° oven for 10 to 15 minutes or till softened. Remove meat from cooker and shred. Return meat to cooker. Stir in lime juice, if desired. To serve fajitas, use a slotted spoon and fill the warmed tortillas with the beef mixture. If desired, add shredded cheese, guacamole, sour cream, and salsa. Roll up tortillas. Makes 6 servings.

Per serving: 426 calories, 29 g protein, 46 g carbohydrate, 13 g total fat (4 g saturated), 53 mg cholesterol, 592 mg sodium, 617 mg potassium

Beef Stroganoff

Tender chunks of beef in a rich herbed sauce ladled over noodles or rice.

1½ pounds beef stew meat, cut into
     1-inch cubes
1 tablespoon cooking oil

2 cups sliced fresh mushrooms
½ cup sliced green onions
2 cloves garlic, minced
½ teaspoon dried oregano, crushed
¼ teaspoon salt
¼ teaspoon dried thyme, crushed
¼ teaspoon pepper
1 bay leaf
1½ cups beef broth (see tip, page 29)
⅓ cup dry sherry

1 8-ounce carton dairy sour cream
½ cup all-purpose flour
¼ cup water

4 cups hot cooked noodles or rice
   Snipped fresh parsley (optional)

1 In a large skillet brown beef, *half* at a time, in hot oil. Drain off fat.

2 In a 3½-quart crockery cooker combine beef, mushrooms, onions, garlic, oregano, salt, thyme, pepper, and bay leaf. Pour beef broth and sherry over all.

3 Cover; cook on low-heat setting for 8 to 10 hours or on high-heat setting for 4 to 5 hours. Discard bay leaf.

4 If using low-heat setting, turn to high-heat setting. Mix together sour cream, flour, and water. Stir about 1 cup of the hot liquid into sour cream mixture. Return all to cooker; stir to combine. Cover and cook on high-heat setting for 30 minutes or till thickened and bubbly.

5 Serve over hot cooked noodles or rice. Sprinkle with snipped fresh parsley, if desired. Makes 6 servings.

Per serving: *497 calories, 36 g protein, 38 g carbohydrate, 20 g total fat (9 g saturated), 135 mg cholesterol, 368 mg sodium, 474 mg potassium*

Ginger Beef and Carrots

This slightly spicy ginger-flavored sauce also goes well over pork or lamb.

1½ **pounds boneless beef round steak, cut into 1-inch cubes**
4 **medium carrots, bias-sliced into ½-inch pieces**
½ **cup bias-sliced green onions**
2 **cloves garlic, minced**
1½ **cups beef broth (see tip, page 29)**
¼ **cup soy sauce**
1 **tablespoon grated gingerroot**
¼ **teaspoon crushed red pepper**

3 **tablespoons cornstarch**
3 **tablespoons cold water**
1 **9-ounce package frozen snap peas, thawed**
1 **4-ounce jar diced pimiento, drained**

3 **cups hot cooked rice**

1 In a 3½- or 4-quart crockery cooker place beef cubes, carrots, green onions, and garlic. In a small bowl combine beef broth, soy sauce, gingerroot, and red pepper; add to the cooker.

2 Cover; cook on low-heat setting for 10 to 12 hours or on high-heat setting for 5 to 6 hours.

3 If using low-heat setting, turn to high-heat setting. In a small bowl stir together cornstarch and water; stir into meat mixture. Cover and cook on high-heat setting for 20 to 30 minutes or till thickened, stirring once. Stir in snap peas and pimiento. Serve over rice. Makes 6 servings.

Per serving: *393 calories, 42 g protein, 37 g carbohydrate, 8 g total fat (3 g saturated), 95 mg cholesterol, 917 mg sodium, 843 mg potassium*

Italian Steak Rolls

Round out the meal with a tossed green salad and a loaf of crusty bread.

1½ to 2 pounds boneless beef round steak

½ cup grated carrot
⅓ cup chopped zucchini
⅓ cup chopped red or green
    sweet pepper
¼ cup sliced green onion
2 tablespoons grated Parmesan cheese
1 tablespoon snipped fresh parsley
1 clove garlic, minced
¼ teaspoon pepper

1 tablespoon cooking oil
1 14-ounce jar meatless spaghetti sauce

6 ounces pasta, cooked and drained

1 Trim fat from meat. Cut meat into 6 portions. Place the meat between 2 pieces of plastic wrap and, with a meat mallet, pound steak to a ⅛- to ¼-inch thickness.

2 In a small bowl combine carrot, zucchini, red or green sweet pepper, green onion, Parmesan cheese, parsley, garlic, and pepper. Spoon ⅙ of the vegetable filling on each piece of meat. Roll up meat around the filling and tie each roll with string or secure with wooden toothpicks.

3 Brown meat rolls on all sides in hot oil. Transfer meat rolls to a 3½- or 4-quart crockery cooker. Pour spaghetti sauce over the meat rolls.

4 Cover; cook on low-heat setting for 7 to 8 hours or on high-heat setting for 3½ to 4 hours. Discard string or toothpicks. Serve meat rolls with hot cooked pasta. Makes 6 servings.

Per serving: 358 calories, 33 g protein, 32 g carbohydrate, 10 g total fat (3 g saturated), 74 mg cholesterol, 341 mg sodium, 474 mg potassium

Hungarian Beef Goulash

Either sweet or hot Hungarian paprika can be used in this goulash.

1½ **pounds beef stew meat, cut into**
   1-inch cubes
1 **tablespoon cooking oil**

2 **medium carrots, bias-sliced into ½-inch**
   pieces
2 **medium onions, thinly sliced**
3 **cloves garlic, minced**
1¼ **cups beef broth (see tip, page 29)**
1 **6-ounce can tomato paste**
1 **tablespoon Hungarian paprika**
1 **teaspoon finely shredded lemon peel**
½ **teaspoon salt**
½ **teaspoon caraway seed**
¼ **teaspoon pepper**
1 **bay leaf**

1 **green sweet pepper, cut into strips**
1 **red or green sweet pepper, cut**
   into strips
3 **cups hot cooked noodles**
   Dairy sour cream or yogurt

1 In a large skillet brown beef, *half* at a time, in hot oil. Drain off fat.

2 Transfer meat to a 3½- or 4-quart crockery cooker. Add carrots, onions, and garlic. In a small bowl combine beef broth, tomato paste, paprika, lemon peel, salt, caraway seed, pepper, and bay leaf. Stir into vegetable-meat mixture.

3 Cover; cook on low-heat setting for 9½ to 11½ hours or on high-heat setting for 3½ to 4½ hours.

4 If using low-heat setting, turn to high-heat setting. Stir in sweet pepper strips. Cover and cook 30 minutes longer on high-heat setting. Discard bay leaf. Serve with hot cooked noodles and a dollop of sour cream or yogurt. Makes 6 servings.

Per serving: 391 calories, 34 g protein, 34 g carbohydrate, 13 g total fat (5 g saturated), 115 mg cholesterol, 442 mg sodium, 745 mg potassium

Sloppy Joes

*Prepare this classic with ground pork or ground
raw chicken or turkey if you're in the mood for a change. Use the
leftovers as topping for the kids' hot dogs.*

1½ **pounds ground beef**
1 **cup chopped onion**
2 **cloves garlic, minced**

¾ **cup catsup**
½ **cup chopped green sweet pepper**
½ **cup chopped celery**
¼ **cup water**
1 **to 2 tablespoons brown sugar**
2 **tablespoons prepared mustard**
2 **tablespoons vinegar**
2 **tablespoons Worcestershire sauce**
1½ **teaspoons chili powder**

8 **hamburger buns, split and toasted**

1 In a large skillet cook ground beef, onion, and garlic till meat is brown and onion is tender. Drain off fat.

2 Meanwhile, in a 3½- or 4-quart crockery cooker combine catsup, green sweet pepper, celery, water, brown sugar, mustard, vinegar, Worcestershire sauce, and chili powder. Stir in meat mixture.

3 Cover; cook on low-heat setting for 6 to 8 hours or on high-heat setting for 3 to 4 hours. Spoon into toasted buns. Makes 8 servings.

Per serving: 340 calories, 21 g protein, 35 g carbohydrate, 13 g total fat (5 g saturated), 53 mg cholesterol, 690 mg sodium, 512 mg potassium

Spaghetti Sauce Italiano

Start this spicy blended sauce in the morning—then
forget about it until dinner!

½ **pound bulk Italian sausage**
¼ **pound ground beef**
½ **cup chopped onion**
1 **clove garlic, minced**

1 **16-ounce can tomatoes, cut up**
1 **8-ounce can tomato sauce**
1 **4-ounce can sliced mushrooms, drained**
½ **cup chopped green sweet pepper**
2 **tablespoons quick-cooking tapioca**
1 **bay leaf**
1 **teaspoon dried Italian seasoning,**
     crushed
⅛ **teaspoon pepper**
   Dash salt

   Hot cooked spaghetti

1 In a skillet cook sausage, ground beef, onion, and garlic till meat is brown and onion is tender. Drain off fat.

2 Meanwhile, in a 3½- or 4-quart crockery cooker combine *undrained* tomatoes, tomato sauce, mushrooms, green sweet pepper, tapioca, bay leaf, Italian seasoning, pepper, and salt. Stir in meat mixture.

3 Cover; cook on low-heat setting for 8 to 10 hours or on high-heat setting for 4 to 5 hours. Discard bay leaf. Serve over hot cooked spaghetti. Makes 4 or 5 servings.

Per serving: 491 calories, 24 g protein, 64 g carbohydrate, 16 g total fat (5 g saturated), 50 mg cholesterol, 1,107 mg sodium, 816 mg potassium

Italian-Style Meat Loaf

*Shape this meat loaf the night before and refrigerate—then pop
it in the cooker the next morning.*

1   **8-ounce can pizza sauce**
1   **beaten egg**
½   **cup chopped onion**
½   **cup chopped green sweet pepper**
⅓   **cup fine dry seasoned bread crumbs**
½   **teaspoon garlic salt**
¼   **teaspoon pepper**
¼   **teaspoon fennel seed,
       crushed (optional)**
1½   **pounds lean ground beef**

½   **cup shredded mozzarella
       cheese (2 ounces)**

1   Reserve ⅓ *cup* pizza sauce; cover and chill.
In a medium mixing bowl combine remaining pizza sauce and egg. Stir in onion, green
sweet pepper, bread crumbs, garlic salt, pepper, and fennel, if desired. Add ground beef
and mix well.

2   Crisscross three 18x2-inch foil strips (atop
a sheet of waxed paper to keep counter
clean). In center of the foil strips shape a 6-inch round meat loaf. Bringing
up foil strips, lift and transfer meat and foil
to a 3½-, 4-, or 5-quart crockery cooker.
Press meat away from sides of the cooker
to avoid burning.

3   Cover; cook on low-heat setting for 7 to
9 hours or on high-heat setting for 3½ to 4½
hours (or to 170° internal temperature).

4   Spread meat with the reserved ⅓ cup
pizza sauce. Sprinkle with mozzarella
cheese. Cover cooker and let stand 5 to 10
minutes.

5   Using foil strips, carefully lift meat loaf
and transfer to a serving plate; discard the
foil strips. Makes 8 servings.

*Per serving: 228 calories, 20 g protein, 8 g carbohydrate, 13 g total fat (5 g saturated), 83 mg cholesterol,
510 mg sodium, 360 mg potassium*

Fennel Pork Roast and Vegetables

Look for fresh fennel from September through April.
Choose firm, smooth bulbs without cracks and brown spots. Bright green
fennel leaves may be used as garnish.

1 2- to 2½-pound boneless pork
    shoulder roast
1 teaspoon fennel seed, crushed
½ teaspoon garlic powder
½ teaspoon dried oregano, crushed
¼ teaspoon pepper
2 tablespoons cooking oil

1½ pounds small red potatoes, halved
1 large fennel bulb, trimmed and cut
    into 1-inch pieces
1½ cups water
2 teaspoons instant chicken
    bouillon granules

½ cup cold water
¼ cup all-purpose flour
    Salt and pepper

1 Trim fat from meat. In a small bowl combine crushed fennel seed, garlic powder, oregano, and pepper. Rub about *1 teaspoon* of the seasoning mixture evenly over roast. In a Dutch oven brown meat on all sides in hot oil. Drain off fat.

2 Place potatoes and fennel in bottom of a 3½- or 4-quart crockery cooker. Sprinkle with remaining seasoning mixture. Stir together the 1½ cups water and bouillon granules; add to cooker. Cut meat, if necessary, to fit into the crockery cooker. Place roast atop vegetable mixture.

3 Cover; cook on low-heat setting for 8 to 10 hours or on high-heat setting for 4 to 5 hours.

4 For gravy, skim fat from juices. Measure 1½ cups juice into a medium saucepan. Stir the ½ cup cold water into the flour; stir into reserved juices in saucepan. Cook and stir till thickened and bubbly. Cook and stir 1 minute more. Season to taste with salt and pepper. Pass gravy with meat. Makes 6 to 8 servings.

Per serving: 439 calories, 30 g protein, 33 g carbohydrate, 20 g total fat (6 g saturated), 99 mg cholesterol, 451 mg sodium, 1,107 mg potassium

Orange-Herbed Pork Roast

Serve with parslied new potatoes and steamed baby carrots.

1 2½- to 3-pound pork sirloin roast
½ teaspoon garlic powder
½ teaspoon ground ginger
½ teaspoon dried thyme, crushed
¼ teaspoon pepper
1 tablespoon cooking oil

1 cup chicken broth (see tip, page 29)
2 tablespoons sugar
2 tablespoons lemon juice
2 teaspoons soy sauce
1½ teaspoons finely shredded orange peel

3 tablespoons cornstarch
½ cup orange juice

1 Trim fat from pork roast. If necessary, cut roast to fit into crockery cooker. In a small bowl combine garlic powder, ginger, thyme, and pepper. Rub spice mixture over entire surface of meat with fingers. In a large skillet brown roast on all sides in hot oil. Drain.

2 Transfer meat to a 3½-, 4-, or 5-quart crockery cooker. Combine chicken broth, sugar, lemon juice, soy sauce, and orange peel; pour over roast.

3 Cover; cook on low-heat setting for 8 to 10 hours or on high-heat setting for 4 to 5 hours.

4 Transfer roast to a serving platter; keep warm. For sauce, pour juices into glass measuring cup. Skim fat. If necessary, add water to equal 2 cups. Transfer to saucepan. Combine cornstarch and orange juice; stir into juices in saucepan. Cook and stir till thickened and bubbly. Cook and stir 2 minutes more. If desired, season to taste. Pass sauce with meat. Makes 8 servings.

Per serving: 197 calories, 29 g protein, 8 g carbohydrate, 6 g total fat (2 g saturated), 78 mg cholesterol, 224 mg sodium, 446 mg potassium

Pork Chops with Apples and Sauerkraut

*Try pork spareribs for a variation of this mouth-watering meal. Rinse and
drain the sauerkraut if you prefer a milder flavor.*

**4 pork sirloin chops, cut ¾ inch thick
     (about 1½ pounds)**
1 tablespoon cooking oil

2 medium potatoes, cut into ¼-inch slices
2 medium carrots, cut into ½-inch pieces
1 medium onion, thinly sliced
1 16-ounce can sauerkraut, drained
**2 small cooking apples, cut into
     ¼-inch slices**
½ cup apple cider or apple juice
¼ cup catsup
½ teaspoon caraway seed

Snipped fresh parsley (optional)

1 In a large skillet brown pork chops on
both sides in hot oil.

2 In a 3½- or 4-quart crockery cooker place
potatoes, carrots, onion, browned pork
chops, sauerkraut, and apples. In a bowl
combine apple cider or apple juice, catsup,
and caraway seed; pour over apples.

3 Cover; cook on low-heat setting for 6
to 8 hours or on high-heat setting for 3 to
4 hours. Garnish with snipped fresh parsley,
if desired. Makes 4 servings.

*Per serving: 413 calories, 28 g protein, 43 g carbohy-
drate, 15 g total fat (4 g saturated), 77 mg cholesterol,
934 mg sodium, 1,064 mg potassium*

Cutting vegetables to size

Vegetables intended for
the crockery cooker are cut
into bite-size pieces not only for
the convenience in eating, but for better cooking, too. Some vegetables can
take longer to cook than meat in
crockery cookers. By
cutting the vegetables into
smaller pieces (about ½ inch
thick), you can be sure they will be
tender and ready to eat when the
meat is done.

Pork Chops and Mustard-Sauced Potatoes

If your meat counter doesn't have ¾-inch-thick chops, ask your butcher to cut a bone-in top loin roast into ¾-inch-thick slices.

6   **pork loin chops, cut ¾ inch thick**
1   **tablespoon cooking oil**

1   **10¾-ounce can condensed cream of mushroom soup**
¼   **cup dry white wine or chicken broth (if using chicken broth see tip, page 29)**
¼   **cup Dijon-style mustard**
1   **teaspoon dried thyme, crushed**
1   **clove garlic, minced**
¼   **teaspoon pepper**
6   **medium potatoes, cut into ¼-inch slices**
1   **medium onion, sliced**

1   In a large skillet brown pork chops on both sides, *half* at a time, in hot oil. Drain off fat.

2   In a large mixing bowl combine soup, wine or chicken broth, mustard, thyme, garlic, and pepper. Add potatoes and onion, stirring to coat. Transfer to a 3½- or 4-quart crockery cooker. Place browned chops atop potatoes.

3   Cover; cook on low-heat setting for 7 to 8 hours or on high-heat setting for 3½ hours. Makes 6 servings.

Per serving: 335 calories, 17 g protein, 39 g carbohydrate, 11 g total fat (3 g saturated), 39 mg cholesterol, 705 mg sodium, 887 mg potassium

Gingered Pork and Prune Dinner

Apples and prunes add a pleasant sweetness to this pork meal.

1 **2-pound boneless pork shoulder roast**
2 **tablespoons cooking oil**

3 **tablespoons quick-cooking tapioca**
2 **medium cooking apples, cored and cut
into ½-inch slices**
4 **medium carrots, bias-sliced into
½-inch pieces**
1 **medium onion, cut into 1-inch chunks**
1 **cup pitted prunes, quartered**

1 **cup chicken broth (see tip, page 29)**
¾ **cup apple juice**
1 **tablespoon lemon juice**
1 **teaspoon ground ginger**
¼ **teaspoon ground cinnamon**
¼ **teaspoon pepper**
⅛ **teaspoon ground cloves**

3 **cups hot cooked couscous or noodles**

1 Trim fat from meat; cut pork into 1-inch cubes. In a large skillet brown pork, *half* at a time, in hot oil. Drain off fat.

2 Transfer pork to a 3½- or 4-quart crockery cooker. Sprinkle tapioca over meat. Add apples, carrots, onion, and prunes.

3 In a small bowl combine chicken broth, apple juice, lemon juice, ginger, cinnamon, pepper, and cloves; pour into cooker.

4 Cover; cook on low-heat setting for 8 to 10 hours or on high-heat setting for 4 to 5 hours. Serve with hot cooked couscous or noodles. Makes 6 servings.

Per serving: 542 calories, 32 g protein, 63 g carbohydrate, 19 g total fat (6 g saturated), 99 mg cholesterol, 268 mg sodium, 951 mg potassium

Aloha Pork Steaks

A sweet and sour pineapple sauce gives these steaks their name.

4 **pork shoulder steaks, cut ½ inch thick**
2 **teaspoons cooking oil**

1 **8-ounce can crushed pineapple**
½ **cup chopped green sweet pepper**
½ **cup water**
⅓ **cup packed brown sugar**
2 **tablespoons quick-cooking tapioca**
2 **tablespoons catsup**
2 **teaspoons soy sauce**
½ **teaspoon dry mustard**

2 **cups hot cooked rice**

1 In a large skillet brown pork steaks on both sides in hot oil. Drain off fat. Transfer steaks to a 3½- or 4-quart crockery cooker.

2 In a bowl combine *undrained* pineapple, green sweet pepper, water, brown sugar, tapioca, catsup, soy sauce, and dry mustard; pour over steaks.

3 Cover; cook on low-heat setting for 6 to 8 hours or on high-heat setting for 3 to 4 hours. Skim fat from sauce. Serve over hot cooked rice. Makes 4 servings.

Per serving: 482 calories, 27 g protein, 57 g carbohydrate, 16 g total fat (5 g saturated), 93 mg cholesterol, 356 mg sodium, 580 mg potassium

Barbecue-Style Ribs

Here's a great way to enjoy ribs without standing over a hot grill! Shred any
left-over meat and serve on buns for sandwiches.

**3 to 3½ pounds pork country-style ribs,
cut crosswise in half and cut into
2-rib portions**

1 cup catsup
½ cup finely chopped onion
¼ cup packed brown sugar
1 tablespoon Worcestershire sauce
½ teaspoon chili powder
½ teaspoon liquid smoke
¼ teaspoon garlic powder
¼ teaspoon bottled hot pepper sauce

1 Preheat broiler. Place ribs on the unheated rack of a broiler pan. Broil 6 inches from the heat till brown, about 10 minutes, turning once. Transfer ribs to a 3½- to 4-quart crockery cooker.

2 In a small bowl combine catsup, onion, brown sugar, Worcestershire sauce, chili powder, liquid smoke, garlic powder, and bottled hot pepper sauce. Pour sauce over ribs, turning to coat.

3 Cover; cook on low-heat setting for 10 to 12 hours or on high-heat setting for 5 to 6 hours.

4 Transfer ribs to a platter. If desired, skim fat from surface of sauce; pour sauce into a medium saucepan. Simmer sauce till reduced and thickened. Pass sauce with ribs. Makes 4 servings.

Per serving: 940 calories, 86 g protein, 33 g carbohydrate, 51 g total fat (18 g saturated), 316 mg cholesterol, 1,115 mg sodium, 1,831 mg potassium

Fruit-Stuffed Ham Loaf

Use a quick-read thermometer to make sure the meat loaf is thoroughly cooked.
The thermometer should register 170°.

¾ **cup mixed dried fruit bits**
2 **tablespoons apple butter**
1 **beaten egg**
¼ **cup milk**
½ **cup graham cracker crumbs**
¼ **teaspoon pepper**
1 **pound ground fully cooked ham**
½ **pound ground pork**

½ **cup packed brown sugar**
2 **tablespoons apple juice**
½ **teaspoon dry mustard**

1 In a small bowl combine fruit bits and apple butter. In a medium bowl combine egg, milk, graham cracker crumbs, and pepper. Add ground ham and pork to egg mixture; mix well.

2 Crisscross three 18x2-inch foil strips (atop a sheet of waxed paper to keep counter clean) (see page 9). In center of the foil strips pat *half* of the meat mixture into a 6-inch circle. Spread fruit mixture on meat circle to within ½ inch of edges. On another sheet of waxed paper pat remaining meat mixture into a 6½-inch circle. Invert atop the first circle. Remove paper. Press edges of meat to seal well. Bringing up foil strips, lift and transfer meat and foil to a 3½-, 4-, or 5-quart crockery cooker. Press meat away from sides of the cooker to avoid burning.

3 Cover; cook on low-heat setting for 6 to 7 hours or on high-heat setting for 3 to 3½ hours.

4 In a small bowl combine brown sugar, apple juice, and dry mustard. Spread over meat. Cover; cook on low-heat or high-heat setting for 30 minutes more.

5 Using foil strips, carefully lift meat loaf and transfer to a serving plate; discard the foil strips. Serve ham loaf with glaze. Makes 6 servings.

Per serving: *336 calories, 22 g protein, 40 g carbohydrate, 10 g total fat (2 g saturated), 91 mg cholesterol, 1,049 mg sodium, 599 mg potassium*

Spiced Lamb Roast and Vegetables

*The unusual combination of spices and flavors add an
exotic richness to this roast.*

1   2½- to 3-pound boneless lamb shoulder
      roast
1   tablespoon cooking oil

1½ pounds whole tiny new potatoes or
      5 medium potatoes

2   cups whole tiny carrots
2   small onions, cut into wedges
1¼ cups beef broth (see tip, page 29)
1   tablespoon honey
1   tablespoon grated gingerroot or
      ¾ teaspoon ground ginger
½   teaspoon salt
½   teaspoon anise seed or ¼ teaspoon
      ground allspice
½   teaspoon ground cinnamon
⅛   to ¼ teaspoon ground red pepper

½   cup cold water
¼   cup all-purpose flour
1½ teaspoons finely shredded orange peel

1 Trim the fat from the lamb roast. If
necessary, cut roast to fit into crockery cooker. In a large skillet brown roast on all sides
in hot oil.

2 Meanwhile, remove a narrow strip of
peel from the center of each new potato, or
peel (if desired) and quarter each medium
potato.

3 In a 3½-, 4-, or 5-quart crockery cooker
place potatoes, carrots, and onions. Place
meat atop vegetables. In a bowl combine
beef broth, honey, gingerroot, salt, anise
seed or allspice, cinnamon, and red
pepper. Pour over meat and vegetables.

4 Cover; cook on low-heat setting for 10 to
12 hours or on high-heat setting for 5 to 6
hours.

5 Remove meat and vegetables with slotted spoon; keep warm. For gravy, skim fat
from juices; measure 1½ cups juices. In a
saucepan, combine cold water, flour, and
orange peel. Stir in the reserved 1½ cups
of juices. Cook and stir till thickened and
bubbly. Cook and stir 1 minute more. If
desired, season to taste. Pass gravy with the
meat and vegetables. Makes 6 to 8 servings.

*Per serving: 462 calories, 37 g protein, 41 g carbohy-
drate, 17 g total fat (5 g saturated), 111 mg cholesterol, 468 mg sodium, 1,039 mg potassium*

Lamb and Vegetable Rice

Add a fresh spinach, cucumber, and tomato salad to complement the meal.

1   2- to 2½-pound boneless lamb shoulder
     roast
1   tablespoon cooking oil

2½ cups hot-style vegetable juice
1   cup regular brown rice
1   teaspoon curry powder
¼   teaspoon salt
2   medium carrots, cut into ½-inch pieces

1   medium green sweet pepper, cut into
     ½-inch-wide strips

1   Trim fat from lamb roast. In a large skillet brown roast on all sides in hot oil.

2   Meanwhile, in a 3½- or 4-quart crockery cooker combine vegetable juice, uncooked rice, curry powder, and salt. Add carrots. Place meat atop carrots.

3   Cover; cook on low-heat setting for 7 to 8 hours or on high-heat setting for 3½ to 4 hours.

4   Add the green sweet pepper to the crockery cooker. Cover and let stand 5 to 10 minutes. Makes 6 servings.

Per serving: 367 calories, 29 g protein, 32 g carbohydrate, 13 g total fat (5 g saturated), 89 mg cholesterol, 544 mg sodium, 611 mg potassium

Lemon-Mustard-Sauced Lamb Dinner

A perfect blend of flavors for lamb roast.

1 2- to 2½-pound boneless lamb
    shoulder roast

½ teaspoon lemon-pepper seasoning
½ teaspoon dry mustard
1 tablespoon cooking oil

4 medium potatoes, quartered
1½ cups whole tiny carrots
1 cup chicken broth (see tip, page 29)
3 tablespoons Dijon-style mustard
2 tablespoons quick-cooking tapioca
1 tablespoon lemon juice
½ teaspoon dried rosemary, crushed
¼ teaspoon finely shredded lemon peel
¼ teaspoon pepper
2 cloves garlic, minced

1 9-ounce package frozen artichoke
    hearts, thawed

1 Trim fat from lamb roast. If necessary, cut roast to fit into crockery cooker. In a small bowl combine lemon-pepper seasoning and dry mustard. Sprinkle evenly over sides of lamb roast; rub lightly with fingers. In a large skillet brown the roast on all sides in hot oil.

2 Meanwhile, in a 3½- or 4-quart crockery cooker place potatoes and carrots. Place meat atop vegetables. In a bowl combine broth, Dijon-style mustard, tapioca, lemon juice, rosemary, lemon peel, pepper, and garlic; pour over all in crockery cooker.

3 Cover; cook on low-heat setting for 10 to 12 hours or on high-heat setting for 4 to 5 hours.

4 If using low-heat setting, turn to high-heat setting. Add thawed artichoke hearts. Cover and cook 30 minutes longer on high-heat setting. Skim fat from gravy and serve with roast. Makes 4 servings.

Per serving: 590 calories, 47 g protein, 52 g carbohydrate, 21 g total fat (7 g saturated), 133 mg cholesterol, 824 mg sodium, 1,488 mg potassium

Lamb Ragout with Couscous

*This is a nicely seasoned lamb dish. Adding vegetables at the end of cooking
helps keep them crisp-tender and fresh-looking.*

1½ to 2 pounds lamb stew meat, cut into
     1-inch pieces
1 tablespoon cooking oil

2 cups coarsely chopped onion
2 medium tomatoes, chopped
2 medium carrots, cut into ½-inch slices
3 cloves garlic, minced
2 tablespoons quick-cooking tapioca
1 cup beef broth (see tip, page 29)
¼ cup dry red wine or water
1 teaspoon dried Italian
     seasoning, crushed
½ teaspoon salt
¼ teaspoon pepper

2 small zucchini, halved lengthwise and
     cut into ¼-inch slices
1 9-ounce package frozen artichoke
     hearts, thawed and quartered

3 cups hot cooked couscous

1 In a large skillet brown lamb, *half* at a
time, in hot oil. Drain off fat.

2 Transfer lamb to a 3½-, 4-, or 5-quart
crockery cooker. Add onion, tomatoes,
carrots, and garlic. Sprinkle with tapioca.
Combine beef broth, wine or water, Italian
seasoning, salt, and pepper; pour into
cooker. Stir to combine.

3 Cover; cook on low-heat setting for 8
to 10 hours or on high-heat setting for 4
to 5 hours.

4 If using low-heat setting, turn to high-
heat setting. Stir in zucchini and thawed
artichoke hearts. Cover and cook 30 minutes longer on high-heat setting. Serve over
hot couscous. Makes 6 servings.

*Per serving: 416 calories, 24 g protein, 43 g carbohy-
drate, 17 g total fat (6 g saturated), 63 mg cholesterol,
435 mg sodium, 860 mg potassium*

Poultry

Chicken Curry

This is a must-try for Indian food lovers!

12 ounces skinless, boneless chicken
  breast halves or thighs

4 medium potatoes, cut into 1-inch
  chunks (1¼ pounds)
1 medium green sweet pepper, cut into
  1-inch pieces (¾ cup)
1 medium onion, sliced

1 cup chopped tomato
1 tablespoon ground coriander
2 teaspoons grated gingerroot or
  ½ teaspoon ground ginger
1½ teaspoons paprika
¾ teaspoon salt
½ to 1 teaspoon crushed red pepper
½ teaspoon ground turmeric
¼ teaspoon ground cinnamon
⅛ teaspoon ground cloves
¾ cup chicken broth (see tip, page 29)

1 tablespoon cornstarch
1 tablespoon cold water

1 Rinse chicken; pat dry. Cut chicken into
1-inch pieces.

2 In 3½- or 4-quart crockery cooker place
potatoes, green sweet pepper, and onion.
Place chicken atop vegetables.

3 For sauce, in a medium bowl combine
tomato, coriander, gingerroot, paprika, salt,
red pepper, turmeric, cinnamon, and cloves;
stir in chicken broth. Pour sauce over chick-
en pieces.

4 Cover; cook on low-heat setting for 8 to
10 hours or on high-setting for 4 to 5 hours.

5 If using low-heat setting, turn to high-
heat setting. Combine cornstarch and water;
stir into broth. Cover and cook 10 to 15
minutes longer on high-heat setting or till
thickened and bubbly. Makes 4 servings.

*Per serving: 288 calories, 22 g protein, 43 g carbohy-
drate, 3 g total fat (1 g saturated), 45 mg cholesterol,
607 mg sodium, 1,065 mg potassium*

Easy Italian Chicken Breasts

Try a variation on this recipe! Substitute boneless,
skinless thighs for the breasts, or use spinach or red sweet pepper fettuccine.
Regular frozen green beans work well, too.

12 ounces skinless, boneless chicken
    breast halves

1 9-ounce package frozen Italian-style
    green beans
1 cup fresh mushrooms, quartered
1 small onion, sliced ¼ inch thick

1 14½-ounce can Italian-style
    stewed tomatoes
1 6-ounce can Italian-style tomato paste
1 teaspoon dried Italian
    seasoning, crushed
2 cloves garlic, minced

4 ounces fettuccine, cooked and drained
    Grated Parmesan cheese (optional)

1 Rinse chicken; pat dry. Cut chicken into 1-inch pieces.

2 In a 3½- or 4-quart crockery cooker place green beans, mushrooms, and onion. Place chicken atop vegetables.

3 In a small bowl combine *undrained* tomatoes, tomato paste, Italian seasoning, and garlic. Pour over chicken.

4 Cover; cook on low-heat setting for 5 to 6 hours or on high-heat setting for 2½ to 3 hours. Serve over hot cooked fettuccine. If desired, pass grated Parmesan cheese. Makes 4 servings.

Per serving: *308 calories, 24 g protein, 44 g carbohydrate, 4 g total fat (1 g saturated), 45 mg cholesterol, 799 mg sodium, 961 mg potassium*

Orange Teriyaki Chicken

*A sauce that's sweet and full of flavor. Garnish the
meal with orange slices or sections.*

1 pound skinless, boneless chicken breast
  halves or thighs
1 16-ounce package loose-pack frozen
  broccoli, baby carrots, and water
  chestnuts
2 tablespoons quick-cooking tapioca

½ cup chicken broth (see tip, page 29)
2 tablespoons brown sugar
2 tablespoons teriyaki sauce
1 teaspoon dry mustard
1 teaspoon finely shredded orange peel
½ teaspoon ground ginger

2 cups hot cooked rice

1 Rinse chicken; pat dry. Cut chicken into
1-inch pieces.

2 In a 3½-, 4-, or 5- quart crockery cooker
place frozen vegetables. Sprinkle tapioca
over vegetables. Place chicken pieces atop
vegetables.

3 For sauce, in a small bowl combine chick-
en broth, brown sugar, teriyaki sauce, mustard, orange peel, and ginger. Pour sauce
over chicken pieces.

4 Cover; cook on low-heat setting for 4 to
6 hours or on high-heat setting for 2 to 3
hours. Serve with hot cooked rice. Serves 4.

*Per serving: 303 calories, 27 g protein, 39 g carbohy-
drate, 4 g total fat (1 g saturated), 60 mg cholesterol,
543 mg sodium, 466 mg potassium*

Spicy Ginger and Tomato Chicken

A superb balance of tomato, ginger, garlic, and crushed red pepper.

1   **2½- to 3-pound cut up boiler-fryer
      chicken, skinned**

2   **16-ounce cans tomatoes**
2   **tablespoons quick-cooking tapioca**
1   **tablespoon grated gingerroot**
1   **tablespoon snipped fresh cilantro
      or parsley**
4   **cloves garlic, minced**
2   **teaspoons brown sugar**
¼   **to 1 teaspoon crushed red pepper**
½   **teaspoon salt**

3   **cups hot cooked couscous or rice**

1   Rinse chicken; pat dry. Place chicken pieces in a 3½- or 4-quart crockery cooker.

2   Drain *1 can* of tomatoes; chop tomatoes from both cans. For sauce, in a medium bowl combine both cans of tomatoes, tapioca, gingerroot, cilantro or parsley, garlic, brown sugar, crushed red pepper, and salt. Pour sauce over chicken.

3   Cover; cook on low-heat setting for 6 to 7 hours or on high-heat setting for 3 to 3½ hours. Skim fat from sauce. Serve sauce with chicken and couscous or rice. Serves 6.

Per serving: 332 calories, 25 g protein, 33 g carbohydrate, 11 g total fat (3 g saturated), 66 mg cholesterol, 507 mg sodium, 593 mg potassium

Southwestern Barbecue-Style Chicken

Serve this south of the border chicken with black beans,
avocado slices, and warmed flour tortillas.

2 to 2½ pounds chicken breasts, thighs, and/or legs, skinned

½ cup tomato sauce
2 tablespoons jalapeño pepper jelly
2 tablespoons lime or lemon juice
2 tablespoons quick-cooking tapioca
1 teaspoon brown sugar
1 teaspoon ground cumin
¼ to ½ teaspoon crushed red pepper

1 Rinse chicken; pat dry. Set chicken aside.

2 In a 3½- or 4-quart crockery cooker combine tomato sauce, jelly, lime or lemon juice, tapioca, brown sugar, cumin, and red pepper. Place chicken pieces atop sauce mixture, meaty side down.

3 Cover; cook on low-heat setting for 6 to 7 hours or on high-heat setting for 3 to 3½ hours. Makes 4 to 6 servings.

Per serving: 227 calories, 26 g protein, 15 g carbohydrate, 7 g total fat (2 g saturated), 81 mg cholesterol, 264 mg sodium, 366 mg potassium

Plum-Spiced Chicken and Vegetables

*The look and taste of a stir-fry dish, only better—you won't
have a lot of last-minute preparation!*

2 to 2½ pounds chicken breasts, thighs,
    and/or legs, skinned

2 cups bias-sliced carrots
2 tablespoons quick-cooking tapioca

1 8-ounce can tomato sauce
½ cup plum jam or preserves
2 tablespoons vinegar
½ teaspoon ground ginger
½ teaspoon ground cinnamon

1 6-ounce package frozen pea
    pods, thawed
3 cups hot cooked rice
¼ cup bias-sliced green onions

1 Rinse chicken; pat dry. Set chicken aside.

2 In a 3½- or 4-quart crockery cooker place
carrots; sprinkle with tapioca. Place chicken
pieces atop carrots.

3 In a bowl combine tomato sauce, plum
jam or preserves, vinegar, ginger, and cinnamon. Pour over chicken pieces.

4 Cover; cook on low-heat setting for 7 to
8 hours or on high-heat setting for 3½ to 4
hours. Stir in thawed pea pods. Arrange
chicken over rice on platter. Skim fat from
sauce; pour over chicken. Sprinkle with
sliced green onions. Makes 6 servings.

*Per serving: 361 calories, 24 g protein, 54 g carbohy-
drate, 5 g total fat (1 g saturated), 61 mg cholesterol,
319 mg sodium, 545 mg potassium*

Italian-Herbed Chicken

Tender chicken pieces with chunks of vegetables produce a Mediterranean-flavored meal perfect over pasta.

2 **to 2½ pounds chicken breasts, thighs, and/or legs, skinned**

2 **cups sliced fresh mushrooms**
1 **14½-ounce can tomato wedges, drained**
1 **9-ounce package frozen artichoke hearts**
½ **cup sliced pitted ripe olives**
3 **tablespoons quick-cooking tapioca**

¾ **cup chicken broth (see tip, page 29)**
¼ **cup dry white wine or chicken broth**
1 **tablespoon dried Italian seasoning, crushed**

4 **ounces linguine, cooked and drained**

1 Rinse chicken; pat dry. Set chicken aside.

2 In a 3½- or 4-quart crockery cooker combine the mushrooms, tomato wedges, frozen artichoke hearts, and olives. Sprinkle with tapioca. Place the chicken pieces atop the vegetables.

3 In a bowl combine the chicken broth, white wine, and Italian seasoning. Pour over the chicken.

4 Cover; cook on low-heat setting for 7 to 8 hours or on high-heat setting for 3½ to 4 hours. Serve with hot cooked linguine. Makes 4 to 6 servings.

Per serving: 397 calories, 35 g protein, 42 g carbohydrate, 10 g total fat (2 g saturated), 81 mg cholesterol, 538 mg sodium, 919 mg potassium

Herbed Chicken and Vegetables

Chicken and vegetables simmered in a delicately wine-flavored sauce.

3 **pounds chicken legs, thighs, or**
   drumsticks, skinned
2 **tablespoons cooking oil**

1 **cup chicken broth (see tip, page 29)**
½ **cup dry white wine**
1 **tablespoon snipped fresh parsley**
½ **teaspoon salt**
½ **teaspoon dried rosemary, crushed**
½ **teaspoon dried thyme, crushed**
¼ **teaspoon pepper**
1 **clove garlic, minced**

4 **medium potatoes, quartered**
4 **medium carrots, cut into ½-inch pieces**
2 **stalks celery, cut into 1-inch pieces**
1 **small onion, sliced**

2 **tablespoons cornstarch**
2 **tablespoons cold water**

1 Rinse chicken; pat dry. In a skillet brown chicken pieces, half at a time, in hot oil.

2 In a bowl combine the chicken broth, wine, parsley, salt, rosemary, thyme, pepper, and garlic.

3 In a 3½-, 4-, or 5-quart crockery cooker place potatoes, carrots, celery, and onion. Place chicken pieces atop vegetables. Pour broth mixture over chicken.

4 Cover; cook on low-heat setting for 8 to 9 hours or on high-heat setting for 4 to 4½ hours.

5 Using a slotted spoon, remove chicken and vegetabes to a platter. Keep chicken and vegetables warm.

6 For gravy, skim fat from cooking juices. Strain juices into saucepan. Combine cornstarch and cold water; stir into juices in saucepan. Cook and stir till thickened and bubbly. Cook and stir 2 minutes more. Pass the gravy with the chicken and vegetables. Makes 6 servings.

Per serving: *338 calories, 27 g protein, 31 g carbohydrate, 10 g total fat (2 g saturated), 79 mg cholesterol, 416 mg sodium, 802 mg potassium*

Maple-Mustard-Sauced Turkey Thighs

Turkey is not just for Thanksgiving anymore!
Complete this delicious, anytime meal with mashed potatoes
and steamed green beans.

2 to 2½ **pounds turkey thighs**
   (about 2 thighs), skinned

½ **cup maple syrup or**
   maple-flavored syrup
⅓ **cup coarse-grain brown mustard**
1 **tablespoon quick-cooking tapioca**

1 Rinse turkey thighs; pat dry. Place turkey thighs in the bottom of a 3½- or 4-quart crockery cooker.

2 In a small bowl stir together syrup, mustard, and tapioca. Pour over turkey.

3 Cover; cook on low heat setting for 6 to 7 hours or on high-heat setting for 2½ to 3 hours. Makes 6 servings.

Per serving: *263 calories, 28 g protein, 19 g carbohydrate, 8 g total fat (2 g saturated), 81 mg cholesterol, 255 mg sodium, 302 mg potassium*

Smoked Sausage and Beans

If desired, top each serving with a dollop of sour cream or yogurt.

1   15½-ounce can red kidney beans
1   15-ounce can black beans, rinsed and
      drained
1   15-ounce can great northern beans,
      drained
1   15-ounce can butter beans, drained
1   pound fully cooked smoked turkey
      sausage, halved lengthwise and cut
      into ½-inch slices
1½ cups catsup
1   medium green sweet pepper, chopped
½   cup chopped onion
¼   cup packed brown sugar
2   cloves garlic, minced
1   teaspoon Worcestershire sauce
½   teaspoon dry mustard
½   teaspoon bottled hot pepper sauce

1   In a 3½-, 4-, or 5-quart crockery cooker combine *undrained* kidney beans, drained black beans, drained great northern beans, butter beans, sausage, catsup, green sweet pepper, onion, brown sugar, garlic, Worcestershire sauce, dry mustard, and hot pepper sauce. Stir all ingredients together.

2   Cover; cook on low-heat setting for 8 to 10 hours or on high-heat setting for 4 to 5 hours. Makes 8 servings.

Per serving: 372 calories, 24 g protein, 58 g carbohydrate, 8 g total fat (0 g saturated), 30 mg cholesterol, 1,499 mg sodium, 852 mg potassium

Turkey Meatballs and Gravy

No one will believe this rich tasting gravy starts with a mix.

2 **beaten eggs**
¾ **cup fine dry seasoned bread crumbs**
½ **cup finely chopped onion**
½ **cup finely chopped celery**
2 **tablespoons snipped fresh parsley**
¼ **teaspoon pepper**
⅛ **teaspoon garlic powder**
2 **pounds ground raw turkey**

1½ **teaspoons cooking oil**

1 **10¾-ounce can reduced-sodium con-
    densed cream of mushroom soup**
1 **cup water**
1 **¹⁵⁄₁₆-ounce envelope turkey gravy mix**
½ **teaspoon finely shredded lemon peel**
½ **teaspoon dried thyme, crushed**
1 **bay leaf**

**Hot cooked mashed potatoes or
    buttered noodles**
Snipped fresh parsley (optional)

1 In a large bowl combine eggs, bread crumbs, onion, celery, 2 tablespoons parsley, pepper, and garlic powder. Add ground turkey and mix well. Shape into 1½-inch balls.

2 In a large skillet brown meatballs, half at a time, in hot oil. If necessary add additional oil. Drain meatballs. Transfer to a 3½- or 4-quart crockery cooker.

3 In a bowl combine soup, water, gravy mix, lemon peel, thyme, and bay leaf. Pour over meatballs.

4 Cover; cook on low-heat setting for 6 to 8 hours or on high-heat setting for 3 to 4 hours. Discard bay leaf. Serve with mashed potatoes or noodles. Sprinkle with additional snipped fresh parsley. Makes 8 servings.

Per serving: 314 calories, 21 g protein, 25 g carbohydrate, 14 g total fat (3 g saturated), 98 mg cholesterol, 916 mg sodium, 357 mg potassium

Meatless

Dilled Barley Vegetable Soup

A touch of dill is the secret to this flavorful, filling
stew that's chock-full of vegetables.

1 **15-ounce can red beans, drained**
1 **10-ounce package frozen**
      whole kernel corn
½ **cup medium pearl barley**
1 **14½-ounce can stewed tomatoes**
2 **cups sliced fresh mushrooms**
1 **cup chopped onion**
1 **medium carrot, coarsely**
      chopped
1 **stalk celery, coarsely chopped**
3 **cloves garlic, minced**
2 **teaspoons dried dillweed**
¼ **teaspoon pepper**
1 **bay leaf**
5 **cups vegetable broth or**
      chicken broth (see tip, page 29)

1 In a 3½-, 4-, or 5- quart crockery cooker place beans, corn, barley, *undrained* tomatoes, mushrooms, onion, carrot, celery, garlic, dillweed, pepper, and bay leaf. Pour broth over all.

2 Cover; cook on low-heat setting for 8 to 10 hours or on high-heat setting for 4 to 5 hours.

3 Discard bay leaf. Makes 6 servings.

Per serving: 191 calories, 10 g protein, 45 g carbohydrate, 2 g total fat (0 g saturated), 0 mg cholesterol, 1,111 mg sodium, 632 mg potassium

Vegetable Stock

This is the perfect base for many meatless soups and stews.
Store portions in your freezer for up to three months.

2 **tomatoes, chopped**
2 **medium onions, cut up**
4 **medium carrots, cut up**
1 **turnip or 2 parsnips, cut up**
1 **medium stalk celery with leaves, cut up**
1 **medium potato, halved lengthwise and**
    cut into ½-inch slices
6 **unpeeled cloves garlic**
6 **sprigs parsley**
¾ **teaspoon salt**
½ **teaspoon dried thyme, crushed**
¼ **teaspoon whole black pepper**
1 **bay leaf**
6 **cups water**

1 In a 3½-, 4-, or 5-quart crockery cooker combine the tomatoes, onions, carrots, turnip or parsnips, celery, potato, garlic, parsley, salt, thyme, pepper, and bay leaf. Stir in the water.

2 Cover; cook on low-heat setting for 8 to 10 hours or on high-heat setting for 4 to 5 hours. Strain stock through a large sieve or colander lined with 2 layers of 100 percent cotton cheesecloth. Discard the solids. Makes 6 cups stock. To freeze stock see directions on page 10.

Per 1 cup stock: 44 calories, 1 g protein, 10 g carbohydrate, 0 g total fat (0 g saturated), 0 mg cholesterol, 319 mg sodium, 253 mg potassium

Cheesy Vegetable Soup

Serve this rich, creamy soup with a crisp salad and crunchy breadsticks.

1 16½-ounce can cream-style corn
1 cup chopped, peeled potatoes
½ cup shredded carrot
½ cup chopped onion
½ teaspoon celery seed
¼ teaspoon pepper
2 14½-ounce cans vegetable broth or
     chicken broth (3½ cups)
     (see tip, page 29)

1½ cups shredded American
      cheese (6 ounces)

1 In a 3½-, 4-, or 5-quart crockery cooker combine corn, potatoes, carrot, onion, celery seed, and pepper. Add vegetable or chicken broth.

2 Cover; cook on low-heat setting for 10 to 11 hours or on high-heat setting for 4 to 4½ hours.

3 If using low-heat setting, turn to high-heat setting. Stir cheese into hot soup. Cover and cook on high-heat setting 30 to 60 minutes longer or till cheese is melted. Makes 4 servings.

Per serving: 291 calories, 14 g protein, 38 g carbohydrate, 11 g total fat (6 g saturated), 25 mg cholesterol, 1,575 mg sodium, 651 mg potassium

Lentil Soup

Lentils and vegetables combine to make a thick and satisfying soup.

1   **cup dry lentils**
1   **cup chopped carrot**
1   **cup chopped celery**
1   **cup chopped onion**
2   **cloves garlic, minced**
½   **teaspoon dried basil, crushed**
½   **teaspoon dried oregano, crushed**
¼   **teaspoon dried thyme, crushed**
1   **bay leaf**
2   **14½-ounce cans vegetable broth or**
      chicken broth (3½ cups)
      (see tip, page 29)
1½ **cups water**
1   **14½-ounce can Italian-style stewed**
      tomatoes

¼   **cup snipped fresh parsley**
2   **tablespoon cider vinegar (optional)**

1   Rinse lentils. In a 3½-, 4-, or 5-quart crockery cooker place lentils, carrot, celery, onion, garlic, basil, oregano, thyme, and bay leaf. Stir in vegetable or chicken broth, water, and *undrained* tomatoes.

2   Cover; cook on low-heat setting for 12 hours or on high-heat setting for 5 to 6 hours. Discard bay leaf. Stir in parsley and vinegar (if desired). Makes 6 servings.

Per serving: 185 calories, 13 g protein, 32 g carbohydrate, 1 g total fat (0 g saturated), 1 mg cholesterol, 725 mg sodium, 881 mg potassium

Herbed Vegetable Soup

Freeze left-over servings, then reheat for a quick warm-up on a rainy day.

1 10-ounce package frozen Italian-style
      green beans
1 10-ounce package frozen whole kernel
      corn
1 cup chopped onion
1 cup finely chopped carrots
1 cup coarsely chopped zucchini
2 cloves garlic, minced
6 cups vegetable broth, chicken broth, or
      beef broth (see tip, page 29)
1 6-ounce can tomato paste
2 tablespoons snipped fresh parsley
1 teaspoon dried marjoram, crushed
½ teaspoon dried basil, crushed
1 bay leaf

1 4-ounce package small pasta (1½ cups)

1 In a 3½-, 4-, or 5-quart crockery cooker
combine frozen green beans, frozen corn,
onion, carrots, zucchini, and garlic. Add
broth, tomato paste, parsley, mar-joram,
basil, and bay leaf. Stir to combine.

2 Cover; cook on low setting for 7 to 9
hours or high setting for 3 to 4 hours. Add
pasta; cook on low or high heat setting for
1 hour more. Discard bay leaf. Makes 6 to
8 main-dish servings.

*Per serving: 161 calories, 8 g protein, 30 g carbohy-
drate, 2 g total fat (0 g saturated), 1 mg cholesterol,
615 mg sodium, 602 mg potassium*

Zesty Herbed Mushroom-Tomato Sauce

*For a heartier main dish, brown some ground beef
in a skillet and drain off the fat. Add the browned meat
to the tomato mixture before cooking.*

2 **16-ounce cans whole tomatoes, cut up**
2 **cups sliced fresh mushrooms**
1 **6-ounce can tomato paste**
½ **cup chopped onion**
2 **cloves garlic, minced**
2 **tablespoons grated Parmesan cheese**
2 **teaspoons dried oregano, crushed**
2 **teaspoons brown sugar**
1½ **teaspoons dried basil, crushed**
½ **teaspoon salt**
½ **teaspoon fennel seed,
    crushed (optional)**
¼ **to ½ teaspoon crushed red pepper**
1 **bay leaf**

12 **ounces spaghetti, linguini, or other
    pasta, cooked and drained**

    Grated Parmesan cheese (optional)

1 In a 3½- or 4-quart crockery cooker combine *undrained* tomatoes, mushrooms, tomato paste, onion, garlic, grated Parmesan cheese, oregano, brown sugar, basil, salt, fennel seed (if desired), red pepper, and bay leaf.

2 Cover; cook on low-heat setting for 8 to 10 hours or on high-heat setting for 4 to 5 hours.

3 Discard bay leaf. Serve sauce over hot cooked pasta. Top with grated Parmesan cheese, if desired. Makes 6 servings.

Per serving: 310 calories, 12 g protein, 62 g carbohydrate, 2 g total fat (1 g saturated), 2 mg cholesterol, 485 mg sodium, 781 mg potassium

Chunky Vegetable Chili

To reduce hotness, use regular stewed tomatoes and a mild salsa.
Serve with warm cornmeal biscuits. (Pictured on the cover)

1 **medium zucchini, cut into ½-inch pieces**
    (1½ cups)
1 **medium green sweet pepper, coarsely**
    chopped (1 cup)
½ **cup coarsely chopped onion**
½ **cup coarsely chopped celery**
2 **cloves garlic, minced**
2 **to 3 teaspoons chili powder**
1 **teaspoon dried oregano, crushed**
½ **teaspoon ground cumin**
2 **14½-ounce cans Mexican-style stewed**
    tomatoes
1 **17-ounce can whole kernel corn**
1 **15-ounce can black beans,**
    rinsed and drained
1 **8-ounce jar salsa**

Dairy sour cream

1 In a 3½- or 4-quart crockery cooker combine zucchini, green sweet pepper, onion, celery, garlic, chili powder, oregano, and cumin. Stir in *undrained* tomatoes, *undrained* corn, drained beans, and salsa.

2 Cover; cook on low-heat setting for 8 to 10 hours or on high-heat setting for 4 to 5 hours. To serve, ladle the chili into bowls and top with a dollop of sour cream. Makes 4 servings.

Per serving: 277 calories, 13 g protein, 54 g carbohydrate, 7 g total fat (2 g saturated), 6 mg cholesterol, 1,599 mg sodium, 1,440 mg potassium

Vegetable Stew with Cornmeal Dumplings

*Keep an eye on the cooking dumplings through
the clear lid of your crockery cooker. Don't be tempted to open the
lid or the biscuits will be slow to cook.*

3 cups peeled butternut or acorn squash
    cut into ½-inch pieces
2 cups sliced fresh mushrooms
2 14½-ounce cans Italian-style
    stewed tomatoes
1 15-ounce can great northern
    beans, drained
1 9-ounce package frozen Italian-style
    green beans or frozen cut
    green beans
4 cloves garlic, minced
1 cup water
2 teaspoons dried Italian
    seasoning, crushed
¼ teaspoon pepper

½ cup all-purpose flour
⅓ cup cornmeal
2 tablespoons grated Parmesan cheese
1 tablespoon snipped fresh parsley
1 teaspoon baking powder
1 beaten egg
2 tablespoons milk
2 tablespoons cooking oil
    Paprika

1 In a 3½-, 4-, or 5-quart crockery cooker combine squash, mushrooms, *undrained* tomatoes, great northern beans, Italian-style or cut green beans, and garlic. Combine water, Italian seasoning, and pepper. Pour over vegetables.

2 Cover; cook on low-heat setting for 8 to 10 hours or on high-heat setting for 4 to 5 hours.

3 Meanwhile, for dumplings, in a medium-mixing bowl stir together flour, cornmeal, grated Parmesan cheese, parsley, and baking powder. Combine egg, milk, and oil. Add to the flour mixture; stir with a fork just till combined.

4 If using low-heat setting, turn to high-heat setting. Stir the stew to break up squash slightly and to thicken broth. Drop the dumpling mixture by tablespoons onto stew. Sprinkle with paprika.

5 Cover and cook 50 minutes more on high-heat setting (do not lift cover). Makes 6 servings.

Per serving: 255 calories, 11 g protein, 44 g carbohydrate, 7 g total fat (1 g saturated), 38 mg cholesterol, 655 mg sodium, 886 mg potassium

Spicy Black Beans and Rice

As an option, try other pepper varieties,
such as serrano, Anaheim (banana), or small poblano peppers.
Leave the seeds in the peppers for a hotter dish.

2 cups dry black beans

1 cup chopped onion
1 cup chopped celery
1 cup chopped carrot
1 medium yellow or green sweet
    pepper, chopped
2 jalapeño peppers, chopped
4 cloves garlic, minced
1 tablespoon ground cumin
1 teaspoon ground coriander
1 teaspoon dried thyme, crushed
½ teaspoon salt
¼ teaspoon pepper
2 bay leaves
5 cups chicken broth (see tip, page 29)

4 cups hot cooked rice

1 Rinse beans; place in a large saucepan. Add enough water to cover beans by 2 inches. Bring to boiling; reduce heat. Simmer for 2 minutes. Remove from heat and let stand, covered, for 1 hour. (Or, omit simmering and soak beans in cold water overnight in a covered pan.) Drain beans.

2 In a 3½-, 4-, or 5-quart crockery cooker combine onion, celery, carrot, yellow or green sweet pepper, jalapeño peppers, garlic, cumin, coriander, thyme, salt, pepper, and bay leaves. Stir in drained beans and chicken broth.

3 Cover; cook on low-heat setting for 8 to 10 hours or on high-heat setting for 4 to 5 hours. Discard bay leaves. If desired, mash beans slightly with a potato masher. Serve with hot rice. Makes 8 servings.

Per serving: 198 calories, 10 g protein, 38 g carbohydrate, 2 g total fat (0 g saturated), 1 mg cholesterol, 789 mg sodium, 480 mg potassium

Sloppy Vegetable Sandwiches

*Instead of sandwiches, serve the vegetable
mixture on tostada shells with shredded lettuce and
chopped tomato for a taco-style salad.*

1 **cup chopped carrot**
1 **cup chopped celery**
⅔ **cup dry lentils, rinsed and drained**
⅔ **cup regular brown rice**
½ **cup chopped onion**
1 **clove garlic, minced**
2 **tablespoons brown sugar**
2 **tablespoons prepared mustard**
3½ **cups vegetable broth or chicken broth**
    (see tip, page 29)

1 **8-ounce can tomato sauce**
2 **tablespoons vinegar**

8 **whole wheat buns or French rolls, split**
    and toasted

1 In a 3½- or 4-quart crockery cooker combine carrot, celery, dry lentils, uncooked
brown rice, onion, garlic, brown sugar, and
mustard. Stir in vegetable or chicken broth.

2 Cover; cook on low-heat setting for 8
to 10 hours or on high-heat setting for
4 to 5 hours.

3 Stir in tomato sauce and vinegar; cover
and cook 30 minutes more.

4 To serve, spoon mixture onto toasted
buns or rolls. Makes 8 servings.

*Per serving: 271 calories, 11 g protein, 52 g carbohy-
drate, 4 g total fat (1 g saturated), 0 mg cholesterol,
864 mg sodium, 489 mg potassium*

Sweet and Sour Cabbage Rolls

Each person will get two cabbage rolls along with some
shredded cabbage mixture from this dish.

1 large head green cabbage

1 15-ounce can black beans or red kidney
    beans, rinsed and drained
1 cup cooked brown rice
½ cup chopped carrots
½ cup chopped celery
½ cup chopped onion
1 clove garlic, minced
1 32-ounce jar marinara sauce or
    meatless spaghetti sauce

⅓ cup light or dark raisins
3 tablespoons lemon juice
1 tablespoon brown sugar

1 Remove 8 large outer leaves from head of cabbage. In a large saucepan of boiling water cook cabbage leaves about 4 to 5 minutes or just till limp. Drain cabbage leaves.

Trim the thick rib in center of leaf. Set leaves aside. Shred 4 cups of the remaining cabbage and place shredded cabbage in a 3½- or 4-quart crockery cooker.

2 In medium bowl combine beans, cooked rice, carrots, celery, onion, garlic, and ½ cup of the marinara sauce. Divide bean mixture evenly among the 8 cabbage leaves, using about ⅓ cup per leaf. Fold sides of leaf over filling and roll up.

3 Combine remaining marinara sauce, raisins, lemon juice, and brown sugar. Pour about half of the sauce mixture over shredded cabbage in crockery cooker. Stir to mix. Place cabbage rolls atop shredded cabbage. Top with remaining sauce.

4 Cover; cook on low-heat setting for 6 to 8 hours or on high-heat setting for 3 to 4 hours. Carefully remove the cooked cabbage rolls and serve with the shredded cabbage. Makes 4 servings.

Per serving: 423 calories, 14 g protein, 71 g carbohydrate, 13 g total fat (1 g saturated), 0 mg cholesterol, 1,555 mg sodium, 1,761 mg potassium

Vegetable-Barley Medley

This high-fiber dish is delicious and satisfying.

1   15-ounce can black beans, rinsed
        and drained
1   10-ounce package frozen whole
        kernel corn
1   cup chopped onion
½   cup regular pearl barley
1   medium green sweet pepper,
        chopped (¾ cup)
1   medium carrot, thinly sliced (½ cup)
2   cloves garlic, minced
1   14½-ounce can vegetable broth
        chicken broth (1¾ cups) (see tip,
        page 29)
2   tablespoons snipped fresh parsley
1   teaspoon dried basil, crushed, or
        ½ teaspoon dried oregano, crushed
½   teaspoon salt
¼   teaspoon pepper

1   medium zucchini, halved lengthwise
        and thinly sliced
2   medium tomatoes, coarsely chopped
1   tablespoon lemon juice

1   In a 3½-, 4-, or 5-quart crockery cooker place drained beans, corn, onion, barley, green sweet pepper, carrot, and garlic. In a medium bowl combine vegetable or chicken broth, parsley, basil or oregano, salt, and pepper. Stir into vegetable mixture.

2   Cover; cook on low-heat setting for 7 to 8 hours or on high-heat setting for 3½ to 4 hours.

3   If using low-heat setting, turn to high-heat setting. Stir in the zucchini, tomatoes, and lemon juice. Cover and cook 30 minutes longer on high-heat setting. Makes 4 servings.

Per serving: *302 calories, 18 g protein, 60 g carbohydrate, 3 g total fat (1 g saturated), 1 mg cholesterol, 1,199 mg sodium, 1,091 mg potassium*

Eggplant-Tomato Stew with Garbanzo Beans

*Garbanzo beans are also known as chick-peas.
Look for them in the Mexican foods section of your grocery
store or next to the canned beans.*

1 **medium eggplant, peeled and cut into
½-inch cubes**
2 **cups chopped tomatoes**
1½ **cups sliced carrots**
1 **15-ounce can garbanzo beans, drained**
1 **8-ounce can red kidney beans, rinsed
and drained**
1 **cup chopped onion**
1 **cup sliced celery**
3 **cloves garlic, minced**

3 **cups vegetable broth or chicken broth
(see tip, page 29)**
1 **6-ounce can Italian-style tomato paste**
½ **teaspoon dried oregano, crushed**
½ **teaspoon dried basil, crushed**
¼ **teaspoon salt**
¼ **teaspoon pepper**
¼ **teaspoon crushed red pepper**
1 **bay leaf**

1 In a 3½-, 4-, or 5-quart crockery cooker combine eggplant, tomatoes, carrots, garbanzo beans, kidney beans, onion, celery, and garlic.

2 Combine vegetable or chicken broth, tomato paste, oregano, basil, salt, pepper, crushed red pepper, and bay leaf. Pour over vegetables.

3 Cover; cook on low-heat setting for 7 to 8 hours or on high-heat setting for 3½ to 4 hours. Discard bay leaf. Makes 6 servings.

Per serving: 208 calories, 9 g protein, 43 g carbohydrate, 3 g total fat (0 g saturated), 0 mg cholesterol, 1,288 mg sodium, 1,046 mg potassium

Vegetable Curry

*A curry is an Indian or Far Eastern dish that features foods seasoned with
curry powder—a blend of 16 to 20 ground spices.*

4 medium carrots, bias-sliced into ½-inch
   slices (2 cups)
2 medium potatoes, cut into ½-inch
   cubes (2 cups)
1 15-ounce can garbanzo beans, drained
8 ounces green beans, cut into 1-inch
   pieces (1¾ cups)
1 cup coarsely chopped onion
3 cloves garlic, minced
2 tablespoons quick-cooking tapioca
2 teaspoons curry powder
1 teaspoon ground coriander
½ teaspoon crushed red pepper
   (optional)
¼ teaspoon salt
⅛ teaspoon ground cinnamon
1 14½-ounce can vegetable broth or
   chicken broth (1¾ cups) (see tip,
   page 29)

1 16-ounce can tomatoes, cut up
2 cups hot cooked rice

1 In a 3½-, 4-, or 5-quart crockery cooker combine carrots, garbanzo beans, potatoes, green beans, onion, garlic, tapioca, curry powder, coriander, red pepper (if desired), salt, and cinnamon. Pour broth over all.

2 Cover; cook on low-heat setting for 8 to 10 hours or on high-heat setting for 4 to 5 hours. Stir in *undrained* tomatoes. Cover; let stand 5 minutes. Serve with cooked rice. Makes 4 servings.

Per serving: 420 calories, 15 g protein, 84 g carbohydrate, 4 g total fat (0 g saturated), 0 mg cholesterol, 1,124 mg sodium, 1,378 mg potassium

Vegetables & Side Dishes

Spicy Pumpkin Soup

This is a warming soup that's perfect for a chilly autumn day. Look for pumpkin seeds (pepitas) in larger supermarkets or health food stores.

1 **16-ounce can pumpkin**
1 **cup chopped celery**
½ **cup chopped carrot**
½ **cup chopped onion**
½ **teaspoon salt**
½ **teaspoon dried oregano, crushed**
½ **teaspoon dried rosemary, crushed**
¼ **teaspoon ground red pepper**
4 **cups vegetable broth or chicken broth (see tip, page 29)**

2 **medium tomatoes, peeled and chopped, or one 8-ounce can tomatoes, cut up**
   Dairy sour cream or plain yogurt (optional)
   Shelled pumpkin or sunflower seeds (optional)

1 In a 3½- or 4-quart crockery cooker place pumpkin, celery, carrot, onion, salt, oregano, rosemary, and ground red pepper. Gradually stir in vegetable or chicken broth.

2 Cover; cook on low-heat setting for 6 to 8 hours or on high-heat setting for 3 to 4 hours. Stir in chopped tomatoes or *undrained* canned tomatoes. Ladle into bowls. Add a dollop of sour cream and sprinkle with seeds, if desired. Makes 6 to 8 side-dish servings.

Per serving: 56 calories, 2 g protein, 15 g carbohydrate, 1 g total fat (0 g saturated), 0 mg cholesterol, 918 mg sodium, 408 mg potassium

Crockery Dressing

*When you're preparing the holiday dinner, the oven
is full, and you don't want to prepare the stuffing in a turkey,
fix this crockery-cooked version.*

12 **cups dry bread cubes
(see note, page 112)**
2 **cups sliced celery**
½ **cup finely chopped onion**
¼ **cup snipped fresh parsley**
1½ **teaspoons dried sage, crushed**
½ **teaspoon dried marjoram, crushed**
¼ **teaspoon pepper**

1½ **cups chicken broth (see tip, page 29)**
¼ **cup margarine or butter, melted**

1 In a large bowl combine the dry bread
cubes, celery, onion, parsley, sage, marjoram, and pepper.

2 Pour chicken broth and margarine or
butter over bread mixture and toss gently.
Place bread mixture in a 3½-, 4-, or 5-quart
crockery cooker.

3 Cover; cook on low heat setting for 4 to 5
hours. Makes 8 to 10 servings.

*Per serving: 253 calories, 7 g protein, 37 g carbohy-
drate, 9 g total fat (2 g saturated), 0 mg cholesterol,
568 mg sodium, 355 mg potassium*

Hot German Potato Salad

*This salad is a great accompaniment to pork.
It's also great to take to a potluck supper.*

**6 cups peeled potatoes, cut into ¼-inch
  slices (about 2 pounds)**
1 cup chopped onion
1 cup chopped celery

1 cup water
⅔ cup cider vinegar
¼ cup sugar
2 tablespoons quick-cooking tapioca
1 teaspoon salt
¾ teaspoon celery seed
¼ teaspoon pepper

**6 slices bacon, crisp-cooked, drained,
  and crumbled**
¼ cup snipped fresh parsley

1 In a 3½- or 4-quart crockery cooker combine potatoes, onion, and celery.

2 In a bowl combine water, vinegar, sugar, tapioca, salt, celery seed, and pepper. Pour over potatoes.

3 Cover; cook on low-heat setting for 8 to 10 hours or on high-heat setting for 4 to 5 hours. Stir in bacon and parsley. Makes 8 servings.

Per serving: 162 calories, 4 g protein, 33 g carbohydrate, 3 g total fat (1 g saturated), 4 mg cholesterol, 371 mg sodium, 482 mg potassium

New England Crock-Style Baked Beans

*No need to heat up your kitchen by turning the oven on—the crockery
cooker is the perfect partner for fabulous baked beans.*

1 **pound dry navy beans or dry great
    northern beans (2⅓ cups)**
8 **cups cold water**

1 **cup chopped onion**
¼ **pound salt pork, chopped, or 6 slices
    bacon, cooked, drained, and
    crumbled**
1 **cup water**
½ **cup molasses**
⅓ **cup packed brown sugar**
1 **teaspoon dry mustard**
¼ **teaspoon pepper**

1 Rinse beans; drain. In a large saucepan
or Dutch oven combine beans and the
8 cups water. Bring to boiling; reduce heat.
Simmer, covered, for 1½ to 2 hours or till
beans are tender.

2 Drain beans. In a 3½- or 4-quart crockery cooker combine drained beans, onion,
and salt pork or bacon. Add 1 cup water,
molasses, brown sugar, dry mustard, and
pepper. Stir to combine.

3 Cover; cook on low-heat setting for 10 to
12 hours or on high-heat setting for 5 to 6
hours. Stir before serving. Serves 12.

*Per serving: 257 calories, 8 g protein, 39 g carbohy-
drate, 8 g total fat (3 g saturated), 8 mg cholesterol,
145 mg sodium, 495 mg potassium*

Fruit and Pecan Stuffing

Cooking the stuffing in the crockery cooker frees the oven for other dishes.

½ **cup orange liqueur or water**
1 **6-ounce package mixed dried**
     fruit bits (1½ cups)

1 **cup finely chopped celery**
½ **cup sliced green onion**
½ **cup margarine or butter**
2 **tablespoons snipped fresh parsley**
1 **teaspoon dried sage, crushed**
½ **teaspoon dried thyme, crushed**
½ **teaspoon dried marjoram, crushed**
½ **teaspoon salt**
¼ **teaspoon pepper**

10 **cups dry bread cubes***
½ **cup broken pecans, toasted**
1½ **to 2 cups chicken broth**

1 In a small saucepan heat liqueur or water till boiling. Stir in dried fruit. Remove from heat; cover and let stand 10 to 15 minutes.

2 Meanwhile, in a medium saucepan cook celery and onion in margarine or butter over medium heat till tender but not brown; remove from heat. Stir in parsley, sage, thyme, marjoram, salt, and pepper.

3 Place dry bread cubes in a large bowl. Add *undrained* fruit, vegetable mixture, and pecans. Drizzle with enough of the broth to moisten, tossing lightly. Transfer stuffing mixture to a 3½- or 4-quart crockery cooker.

4 Cover; cook on low-heat setting for 5 to 6 hours or on high-heat setting for 2½ to 3 hours. Makes 10 to 12 servings.

***Note:** To prepare dry bread cubes, start with about 20 slices of bread for the 10 cups dry cubes. Cut the bread into ½-inch cubes and spread in a single layer in a large roasting pan. Bake in a 300° oven for 10 to 15 minutes or till dry; stir twice.

Per serving: 282 calories, 4 g protein, 32 g carbohydrate, 14 g total fat (2g saturated), 0 mg cholesterol, 504 mg sodium, 282 mg potassium

Maple Ginger Bean Bake

Sweet and tangy! Use any bean combination with delicious results.

3 15-ounce cans great northern beans
    and/or red kidney beans, pinto
    beans, black beans, butter beans,
    rinsed and drained
1 8-ounce can tomato sauce
¾ cup maple-flavored syrup
¾ cup diced fully-cooked ham or
    Canadian-style bacon (3½ ounces)
2 tablespoons prepared mustard
2 tablespoons vinegar
1 teaspoon grated gingerroot
¼ teaspoon pepper

1 In a 3½- or 4-quart crockery cooker combine beans, tomato sauce, maple-flavored syrup, ham, mustard, vinegar, gingerroot, and pepper.

2 Cover; cook on low-heat setting for 5 to 6 hours or on high-heat setting for 2½ to 3 hours. Makes 8 to 10 servings.

Per serving: 253 calories, 14 g protein, 51 g carbohydrate, 1 g total fat (0 g saturated), 7 mg cholesterol, 936 mg sodium, 416 mg potassium

Coconut-Pecan Sweet Potatoes

*Need more servings for a holiday meal? Double the ingredients
and cook them in a 5- or 6-quart crockery cooker.*

**2 pounds sweet potatoes, peeled
    and shredded**
⅓ cup packed brown sugar
¼ cup margarine or butter, melted
¼ cup coconut
¼ cup broken pecans, toasted
¼ teaspoon ground cinnamon

¼ teaspoon coconut flavoring
¼ teaspoon vanilla
    Toasted coconut (optional)

1 In a 3½-quart crockery cooker combine sweet potatoes, brown sugar, margarine or butter, coconut, pecans, and cinnamon.

2 Cover; cook on low-heat setting for 6 to 8 hours or on high-heat setting for 3 to 4 hours. Stir in coconut flavoring and vanilla. Sprinkle with toasted coconut, if desired. Makes 4 to 6 servings.

Per serving: 408 calories, 4 g protein, 61 g carbohydrate, 18 g total fat (4 g saturated), 0 mg cholesterol, 157 mg sodium, 715 mg potassium

Creamy Succotash

A creamy, colorful blend of vegetables that rounds out a homey dinner.

1 cup dry lima beans
1 16-ounce package frozen whole
    kernel corn
1 cup coarsely chopped red or green
    sweet pepper
½ cup chopped onion
½ cup sliced celery
2 cloves garlic, minced
¼ teaspoon pepper
1 bay leaf
1 10¾-ounce can condensed cream of
    celery soup
1 cup water

6 slices bacon, crisp-cooked, drained,
    and crumbled

1 Rinse beans; drain. In a 3½- or 4-quart crockery cooker combine beans, corn, sweet pepper, onion, celery, garlic, pepper, and bay leaf. In a bowl combine soup and water. Add to cooker.

2 Cover; cook on low-heat setting for 8 to 10 hours or on high-heat setting for 4 to 5 hours. Discard bay leaf. Stir in bacon. Makes 6 servings.

Per serving: 255 calories, 12 g protein, 40 g carbohydrate, 7 g total fat (2 g saturated), 10 mg cholesterol, 486 mg sodium, 753 mg potassium

Quick Fix-Ups

Wild Rice and Chicken Soup

To reduce the sodium content, use a low-sodium soup
and broth. Make your own broth by using the recipe on page 26.

1 **10¾-ounce can condensed cream
of mushroom soup or cream of
chicken soup**
2½ **cups chopped cooked chicken**
2 **cups sliced fresh mushrooms**
1 **cup coarsely shredded carrot**
1 **cup sliced celery**
1 **6-ounce package long grain and wild
rice mix**
5 **cups chicken broth (see tip, page 29)**
5 **cups water**

1 In a 5- or 6-quart crockery cooker combine soup, chicken, mushrooms, carrot, celery, rice, and contents of seasoning packet. Gradually stir in broth and water.

2 Cover; cook on low-heat setting for 6 hours or on high-heat setting for 3 hours. Makes 8 to 10 servings.

Per serving: 241 calories, 21 g protein, 24 g carbohydrate, 7 g total fat (2 g saturated), 46 mg cholesterol, 1,237 mg sodium, 443 mg potassium

Sausage and Tortellini Soup

This recipe goes together in a snap and yields a soup that's deserving of guests.
Serve with tasty submarine sandwiches.

6 ounces fully cooked smoked turkey
    sausage, halved lengthwise and cut
    into ½-inch slices
2 cups pre-shredded coleslaw mix
1 cup loose-pack frozen cut green beans
    or Italian-style green beans
2 14½-ounce cans Italian-style
    stewed tomatoes
1 10½-ounce can condensed French
    onion soup
3 cups water

1 9-ounce package refrigerated fresh
    cheese-filled tortellini
    Grated Parmesan cheese

1 In a 3½-, 4-, or 5-quart crockery cooker place sausage, coleslaw mix, green beans, *undrained* tomatoes, soup, and water.

2 Cover; cook on low-heat setting for 8 to 10 hours or on high-heat setting for 4 to 5 hours.

3 If using low-heat setting, turn to high-heat setting. Stir in tortellini. Cover and cook for 10 to 15 minutes longer on high-heat setting. Ladle soup into bowls. Sprinkle with grated Parmesan cheese. Makes 6 servings.

Per serving: 271 calories, 17 g protein, 37 g carbohydrate, 7 g total fat (2 g saturated), 41 mg cholesterol, 1,390 mg sodium, 666 mg potassium

Quick Vegetable-Beef Soup

A full-flavored soup from just a few ingredients.

1 **pound ground beef**

1 **14½-ounce can beef broth (1¾ cups) (see tip, page 29)**

1¼ **cups water**

1 **10-ounce package frozen mixed vegetables**

1 **14½-ounce can tomatoes, cut up**

1 **11¼-ounce can condensed tomato soup with Italian herbs**

1 **tablespoon dried minced onion**

¼ **teaspoon garlic powder**

1 In a large skillet cook beef till brown. Drain off fat.

2 Transfer meat to a 3½- or 4-quart crockery cooker. Add beef broth, water, frozen vegetables, *undrained* tomatoes, tomato soup, onion, and garlic powder.

3 Cover; cook on low-heat setting for 7 to 8 hours or on high-heat setting for 3½ to 4 hours. Makes 4 to 6 servings.

Per serving: *360 calories, 25 g protein, 28 g carbohydrate, 17 g total fat (6 g saturated), 71 mg cholesterol, 1,118 mg sodium, 757 mg potassium*

Mexican Chicken Chowder

Use the chicken broth recipe on page 26 of this book and a
low-sodium soup to reduce the sodium content.

2½ cups chopped cooked chicken
 1 11-ounce can whole kernel corn with
    sweet peppers, drained
 1 10¾-ounce can condensed cream of
    potato soup
 1 4-ounce can diced green chili peppers
 2 tablespoons snipped fresh cilantro
 1 1¼-ounce envelope taco seasoning mix
 3 cups chicken broth (see tip, page 29)

 1 8-ounce carton dairy sour cream
 ½ of an 8-ounce package cheese spread
    with jalapeño peppers, cubed

1 In a 3½- or 4-quart crockery cooker combine chicken, corn, soup, *undrained* chili peppers, cilantro, and taco seasoning mix. Stir in chicken broth.

2 Cover; cook on low-heat setting for 8 to 10 hours or on high-heat setting for 4 to 5 hours.

3 Stir about 1 cup of the hot soup into sour cream. Stir sour cream mixture and cheese into the mixture in crockery cooker; cover and let stand 5 minutes. Stir till combined. Makes 6 servings.

Per serving: *376 calories, 30 g protein, 21 g carbohydrate, 21 g total fat (10 g saturated), 93 mg cholesterol, 1,986 mg sodium, 520 mg potassium*

Corn and Sausage Chowder

Slow cooking brings out the sausage flavor
of this creamy, hearty soup.

1 **pound fully cooked smoked turkey**
      sausage, halved lengthwise and
      cut into ½-inch slices
3 **cups loose-pack frozen hash brown**
      potatoes with onions and peppers
1 **medium carrot, coarsely chopped**
1 **stalk celery, coarsely chopped**
2 **10¾-ounce cans condensed golden**
      corn soup
2½ **cups water**

  Snipped fresh chives or parsley

1 In a 3½-, 4-,or 5-quart crockery cooker place sausage, frozen hash brown potatoes, carrot, and celery. In a bowl combine soup and water. Add to cooker.

2 Cover; cook on low-heat setting for 8 to 10 hours or on high-heat setting for 4 to 5 hours. Ladle into bowls. Sprinkle with chives or parsley. Makes 6 servings.

Per serving: 275 calories, 16 g protein, 32 g carbohydrate, 8 g total fat (1 g saturated), 52 mg cholesterol, 668 mg sodium, 395 mg potassium

Sweet and Sour Chicken with Almonds

*For variety, use other flavors of cooking sauce and
different mixes of vegetables.*

1 **pound skinless, boneless chicken breast
    halves**

1 **24½-ounce jar sweet and sour cooking
    sauce for chicken**
1 **16-ounce package loose-pack frozen
    broccoli, carrots, water chestnuts,
    and red sweet peppers**

2 **cups hot cooked rice**
¼ **cup toasted, chopped almonds**

1 Rinse chicken; pat dry. Cut chicken into
1-inch pieces.

2 In a 3½- or 4-quart crockery cooker combine chicken, cooking sauce, and frozen
vegetables.

3 Cover; cook on low-heat setting for 5 to 6
hours or on high-heat setting for 2½ to 3
hours. Serve with hot cooked rice. Sprinkle
with almonds. Makes 4 servings.

*Per serving: 415 calories, 27 g protein, 62 g carbohy-
drate, 7 g total fat (1 g saturated), 59 mg cholesterol,
526 mg sodium, 493 mg potassium*

Chicken with Vegetables and Stuffing

*This tastes just like traditional chicken with stuffing—but it's quicker
and easier to prepare. A great use for leftover chicken or turkey.*

1 **6-ounce package chicken flavor
    stuffing mix**

2½ **cups chopped cooked chicken**
2 **cups zucchini, cut into ½-inch pieces**
2 **cups sliced fresh mushrooms**
1 **medium red or green sweet pepper,
    cut into ½-inch pieces**
½ **cup chopped onion**
1 **10¾-ounce can condensed cream
    of chicken soup or cream of
    mushroom soup**

1 Prepare stuffing mix according to
package instructions except reduce water
to ½ cup. (Stuffing will not be completely
moistened.) Set aside.

2 In a large bowl combine chicken, zucchini, mushrooms, red or green sweet pepper,
and onion. Stir in soup.

3 In a 3½-, 4-, or 5-quart crockery cooker
place *half* of the chicken-vegetable mixture;
top with *half* of the stuffing. Repeat layers.

4 Cover; cook on low-heat setting for 5 to
6 hours or on high-heat setting for 2½ to 3
hours. Makes 6 servings.

Per serving: *315 calories, 24 g protein, 29 g carbohydrate, 11 g total fat (3 g saturated), 52 mg cholesterol,
976 mg sodium, 432 mg potassium*

Cheesy Scalloped Potatoes and Ham

A new twist to an old-fashioned favorite.

1 **24-ounce package loose-pack frozen hash brown potatoes with onion and peppers**
2 **cups diced fully cooked ham (10-ounces)**
1 **2-ounce jar diced pimiento, drained**
1 **tablespoon snipped fresh parsley**
¼ **teaspoon pepper**

1 **11-ounce can condensed cheddar cheese soup**
¾ **cup milk**

1 In a 3½-, 4-, or 5-quart crockery cooker combine frozen hash brown potatoes, ham, pimiento, parsley, and pepper.

2 In a medium bowl combine the soup and milk; pour over the potato mixture in the crockery cooker.

3 Cover; cook on low-heat setting for 7 to 9 hours or on high-heat setting for 3½ to 4 hours. Stir before serving. Makes 4 servings.

Per serving: 470 calories, 24 g protein, 42 g carbohydrate, 24 g total fat (11 g saturated), 43 mg cholesterol, 1,454 mg sodium, 960 mg potassium

Cranberry-Raspberry-Sauced Pork Chops

A lovely entrée from simple ingredients.

6 boneless smoked pork chops

1 cup cranberry-orange sauce
½ cup seedless red raspberry preserves
1 teaspoon quick-cooking tapioca
1 teaspoon finely shredded lemon peel
¼ teaspoon ground cardamom

3 fresh apricots or plums, pitted
   and sliced
3 cups hot cooked couscous

1 In a 3½- or 4-quart crockery cooker place pork chops.

2 For sauce, in a small bowl combine cranberry-orange sauce, raspberry preserves, tapioca, lemon peel, and cardamom. Pour over chops.

3 Cover; cook on low-heat setting for 7 to 8 hours or on high-heat setting for 3½ to 4 hours. Stir in sliced fruit. Cover; let stand 5 minutes. Serve with hot couscous. Makes 6 servings.

Per serving: 340 calories, 23 g protein, 50 g carbohydrate, 5 g total fat (1 g saturated), 27 mg cholesterol, 1,040 mg sodium, 449 mg potassium

Desserts

Strawberry-Rhubarb Compote

*This is a real treat when rhubarb and
strawberries are in season, but still wonderful with frozen fruit.
Try it served over individual shortcakes as well.*

**6 cups fresh rhubarb, cut into 1-inch
pieces (about 2 pounds) or one
20-ounce package frozen
unsweetened sliced rhubarb**

1 cup sugar

**½ teaspoon finely shredded orange peel
or lemon peel**

¼ teaspoon ground ginger

3 inches stick cinnamon

**½ cup white grape juice, white
wine, or water**

**2 cups fresh strawberries, halved or
quartered
Vanilla ice cream or frozen yogurt**

1 In a 3½- or 4-quart crockery cooker place rhubarb. In a bowl combine sugar, orange or lemon peel, and ginger; sprinkle over rhubarb. Add cinnamon stick. Pour grape juice, wine, or water over all.

2 Cover; cook on low-heat setting for 5 to 6 hours or on high-heat setting for 2½ to 3 hours.

3 Remove stick cinnamon. If using low-heat setting, turn to high-heat setting. Stir in strawberries. Cover and cook 30 minutes longer on high-heat setting. Spoon the warm compote into dishes. Serve with ice cream or yogurt. Makes 4 to 6 servings.

Per serving: 404 calories, 5 g protein, 84 g carbohydrate, 8 g total fat (5 g saturated), 29 mg cholesterol, 63 mg sodium, 812 mg potassium

Cranberry-Raspberry Fruit Compote

A pretty and elegant fruit dessert. Serve warm or chilled
over angel cake or frozen yogurt.

3 cups cranberry-raspberry drink or
    cranberry juice cocktail
1 8-ounce package mixed dried fruit, cut
    into 1-inch pieces
1 3-ounce package dried
    cranberries or ⅔ cup raisins
½ cup honey
6 inches stick cinnamon
1 tablespoon finely shredded orange peel

1 12-ounce package loose-pack frozen
    red raspberries

1 In a 3½- or 4-quart crockery cooker combine the cranberry-raspberry drink or cranberry juice cocktail, dried fruit, dried cranberries or raisins, honey, stick cinnamon, and orange peel.

2 Cover; cook on low-heat setting for 8 to 10 hours or on high-heat setting for 4 to 5 hours. Stir in frozen raspberries; let stand 10 minutes. Discard cinnamon. Spoon compote into bowls. Makes 6 servings.

Per serving: 327 calories, 2 g protein, 84 g carbohydrate, 1 g total fat (0 g saturated), 0 mg cholesterol, 17 mg sodium, 436 mg potassium

Orange and Rum Apple Compote

Try this yummy, homey dessert over butter brickle ice cream.

6 **cups peeled and cored cooking apples
    cut into ½-inch slices
    (about 2 pounds)**
1 **6-ounce package mixed dried fruit bits**
¼ **cup sugar**
2 **teaspoons finely shredded orange peel**
1 **tablespoon quick-cooking tapioca**
¾ **cup orange juice or apple juice**
3 **tablespoons rum (optional)**

½ **cup whipping cream**
½ **cup toasted, sliced almonds**

1 In a 3½- or 4-quart crockery cooker combine the apples, dried fruit bits, sugar, and orange peel. Sprinkle with tapioca. Add the orange juice or apple juice and the rum (if desired).

2 Cover; cook on low-heat setting for 8 to 10 hours or on high-heat setting for 4 to 5 hours. Spoon compote into bowls. Top each serving with 1 tablespoon cream and sliced almonds. Makes 8 servings.

Per serving: 256 calories, 3 g protein, 45 g carbohydrate, 9 g total fat (4 g saturated), 20 mg cholesterol, 22 mg sodium, 385 mg potassium

Blueberry-Blackberry Cobbler

The cobbler will rise to the top while cooking. To serve, spoon the fruit
from the bottom of the cooker over the warm cake.

1 cup all-purpose flour
¾ cup sugar
1 teaspoon baking powder
¼ teaspoon salt
¼ teaspoon ground cinnamon
¼ teaspoon ground nutmeg
2 slightly beaten eggs
2 tablespoons cooking oil
2 tablespoons milk

1½ cups fresh or frozen blueberries
1½ cups fresh or frozen blackberries
¾ cup sugar
½ cup water
1 teaspoon finely shredded orange peel
  Half-and-half, light cream, whipped
    cream, or ice cream (optional)

1 In a medium mixing bowl stir together flour, ¾ cup sugar, baking powder, salt, cinnamon, and nutmeg. Combine eggs, oil, and milk; add to dry ingredients. Stir just till moistened. Spread batter evenly in the bottom of a 3½- or 4-quart crockery cooker.

2 In a medium saucepan combine blueberries, blackberries, ¾ cup sugar, water, and orange peel; bring to a boil. Pour hot fruit over batter.

3 Cover; cook on high-heat setting for 2 to 2½ hours or till a toothpick inserted into the center of the cake comes out clean. Let stand about 30 minutes to cool slightly before serving.

4 To serve, spoon the warm cobbler into bowls. Serve with cream or ice cream, if desired. Makes 6 servings.

Per serving: 371 calories, 5 g protein, 75 g carbohydrate, 7 g total fat (1 g saturated), 71 mg cholesterol, 177 mg sodium, 154 mg potassium

Orange-Pumpkin Custard

*The crockery cooker virtually eliminates the problem of overcooking, producing
a custard with a deliciously creamy texture.*

2 **slightly beaten eggs**
1 **cup canned pumpkin**
½ **cup sugar**
½ **teaspoon ground cinnamon**
½ **teaspoon finely shredded orange peel**
¼ **teaspoon ground allspice**
1 **12-ounce can evaporated milk**

Whipped cream (optional)
Toasted chopped pecans (optional)

1 In a large mixing bowl combine eggs, pumpkin, sugar, cinnamon, orange peel, and allspice. Stir in evaporated milk. Pour into a 1-quart souffle dish. Cover the dish tightly with foil.

2 Tear off two 15x6-inch pieces of heavy foil. Fold each piece in thirds lengthwise. Crisscross the strips and place the soufflé dish in the center. Bringing up foil strips, lift the ends of the strips and transfer the dish and foil to a 3½-, 4-, or 5-quart crockery cooker. (Leave foil strips under dish.) Pour warm water into the cooker around the dish to a depth of 1½ inches.

3 Cover; cook on low-heat setting about 4 hours or till a knife inserted near the center comes out clean.

4 Using the foil strips, carefully lift the dish out of the cooker. Let stand 20 minutes. Serve warm or chilled. Top each serving with a dollop of whipped cream and pecans, if desired. Makes 4 servings.

Per serving: 271 calories, 10 g protein, 39 g carbohydrate, 9 g total fat (5 g saturated), 132 mg cholesterol, 125 mg sodium, 418 mg potassium

Lemony Strawberry Pears

*Strawberries and lemon team up to make a
light and refreshing sauce for pears. Any leftover strawberry
sauce makes a great ice cream topper.*

5 **medium pears**

1 **16-ounce package frozen
      strawberries, thawed**
⅓ **cup sugar**
1 **teaspoon finely shredded lemon peel**
1 **tablespoon lemon juice**
1 **teaspoon quick-cooking tapioca**
⅛ **teaspoon ground nutmeg**
3 **inches stick cinnamon**

1 Peel pears. Core fruit from the bottom, leaving stems attached. Place pears upright in a 3½- or 4-quart crockery cooker.

2 In a blender container blend strawberries until smooth. Add sugar, lemon peel, lemon juice, tapioca, and nutmeg to pureed strawberries. Pour strawberry mixture over pears in crockery cooker, coating each pear. Add cinnamon stick.

3 Cover; cook on high-heat setting for 2 to 3 hours. Discard cinnamon. Serve pears warm or chilled. Makes 5 servings.

Per serving: 185 calories, 1 g protein, 48 g carbohydrate, 1 g total fat (0 g saturated), 0 mg cholesterol, 2 mg sodium, 348 mg potassium

Caramel-Orange Pudding Cake

*A classic combination—moist, tender cake
smothered in a rich caramel sauce.*

1   cup all-purpose flour
⅓   cup sugar
1   teaspoon baking powder
½   teaspoon finely shredded orange peel
½   teaspoon ground cinnamon
½   cup milk
2   tablespoons cooking oil
½   cup chopped pecans
¼   cup currants or raisins

⅔   cup packed brown sugar
¾   cup water
¾   cup orange juice
1   tablespoon margarine or butter
½   teaspoon finely shredded orange peel

   Half-and-half or light cream

1   In a mixing bowl stir together flour, ⅛ cup sugar, baking powder, ½ teaspoon orange peel, and cinnamon. Add milk and oil. Stir till batter is combined. Stir in pecans and currants or raisins. Spread batter evenly in the bottom of a 3½- or 4-quart crockery cooker.

2   In a small saucepan combine brown sugar, water, orange juice, margarine or butter, and ½ teaspoon orange peel. Bring to a boil; boil 2 minutes. Pour evenly over batter in crockery cooker.

3   Cover; cook on high-heat setting for 2 to 2½ hours or till a toothpick inserted 1-inch deep into center of the cake comes out clean. Let stand 30 to 40 minutes to cool slightly before serving.

4   To serve, spoon the warm cake and pudding into dessert dishes. Serve with half-and-half or light cream. Makes 6 servings.

Per serving: 423 calories, 5 g protein, 61 g carbohydrate, 19 g total fat (5 g saturated), 21 mg cholesterol, 59 mg sodium, 331 mg potassium

Mexican Chocolate Bread Pudding

*Chocolate and cinnamon combine to make a
familiar dessert wonderfully new.*

1½ **cups half-and-half or light cream**
3 **ounces unsweetened chocolate,**
   coarsely chopped
⅓ **cup raisins (optional)**

2 **beaten eggs**
½ **cup sugar**
¾ **teaspoon ground cinnamon**
3 **cups ½-inch bread cubes (about**
   4 slices; see note, page 112)

Whipped cream (optional)
Chopped nuts (optional)

1 In a small saucepan heat cream over
medium heat till steaming. Remove from
heat; add chopped chocolate and raisins.
Stir occasionally till chocolate melts.

2 In a medium bowl whisk together eggs,
sugar, and cinnamon. Whisk in cream mixture. Gently stir in bread cubes. Pour into a
1-quart soufflé dish. Cover the dish tightly
with foil.

3 Tear off two 15x6-inch pieces of heavy
foil. Fold each piece in thirds lengthwise.
Crisscross the strips and place the soufflé
dish in the center. Bringing up foil strips, lift
the ends of the strips and transfer the dish
and foil to a 3½-, 4-, or 5-quart crockery
cooker. (Leave foil strips under dish.) Pour
warm water into the cooker around the dish
to a depth of 2 inches (about 1 cup).

4 Cover; cook on low-heat setting about 4
hours or on high-heat setting about 2 hours
or till a knife inserted near the center comes
out clean.

5 Using foil strips, carefully lift the dish out
of cooker. Serve bread pudding warm or
chilled. If desired, top each serving with a
dollop of whipped cream and sprinkle with
nuts. Makes 6 servings.

Per serving: *281 calories, 7 g protein, 31 g carbohydrate, 17 g total fat (8 g saturated), 95 mg cholesterol,
124 mg sodium, 239 mg potassium*

Mocha-Pecan Pudding Cake

*Pair this double chocolate cake and warm mocha sauce with a
cappucino for the perfect grand finale.*

1 cup all-purpose flour
½ cup sugar
2 tablespoons unsweetened cocoa
    powder
1½ teaspoons baking powder
½ cup milk
2 tablespoons cooking oil
1 teaspoon vanilla
½ cup miniature semisweet chocolate
    pieces
½ cup broken pecans

¾ cup sugar
¼ cup unsweetened cocoa powder
2 teaspoons instant coffee crystals
1½ cups boiling water
¼ cup coffee liqueur (optional)

Vanilla ice cream (optional)

1 In a mixing bowl stir together flour, ½ cup sugar, 2 tablespoons cocoa powder, and baking powder. Add milk, oil, and vanilla. Stir till batter is smooth. Stir in chocolate pieces and pecans. Spread batter evenly in the bottom of a greased 3½- or 4-quart crockery cooker.

2 Combine the ¾ cup sugar and ¼ cup cocoa powder. Dissolve coffee crystals in boiling water; stir in coffee liqueur, if desired. Gradually stir coffee mixture into the sugar-cocoa mixture. Pour evenly over batter in crockery cooker.

3 Cover; cook on high-heat setting for 2 to 2½ hours or till a toothpick inserted 1-inch deep into the center of the cake comes out clean. Let stand 30 to 40 minutes to cool slightly before serving.

4 To serve, spoon the warm cake into dessert dishes, then spoon pudding over the cake. Top with a scoop of vanilla ice cream, if desired. Makes 6 servings.

Per serving: 434 calories, 5 g protein, 72 g carbohydrate, 15 g total fat (1 g saturated), 2 mg cholesterol, 101 mg sodium, 184 mg potassium

Creamy Chocolate-Almond Fondue

You don't need a fondue pot to make this irresistible fondue. Reheat left-overs—if there are any—and serve over ice cream.

2 7-ounce bars milk chocolate, broken into pieces
3 ounces white baking bar, chopped
1 7-ounce jar marshmallow créme
¾ cup whipping cream, half-and-half, or light cream
¼ cup finely chopped toasted almonds

3 tablespoons amaretto (optional)

Pound cake cubes
Assorted fruit, cut into bite-size pieces

1 In a 3½- or 4-quart crockery cooker combine milk chocolate, white baking bar, marshmallow créme, cream, and almonds.

2 Cover; cook on low-heat setting for 2 to 2½ hours or till chocolate melts. Stir till smooth. If desired, stir in amaretto.

3 To serve, spear cake cubes or fruit with fondue forks; dip into chocolate mixture. Makes about 4 cups.

Per ¼ cup fondue with pound cake: 249 calories, 3 g protein, 29 g carbohydrate, 15 g total fat (9 g saturated), 15 mg cholesterol, 46 mg sodium, 134 mg potassium

Use canning jars as baking molds

Create a simple baking or steaming mold with a straight-sided, wide-mouth canning jar. To assure that the baked cake or bread will slip out easily, grease the inside of the jar well. Lining the bottom of the jar with waxed paper also will help.

Grease a piece of foil on one side. Place the greased side down over the top of the jar and press the foil around the edges to seal tightly.

Brownie Cakes

*Even more delicious if you drizzle hot fudge topping
over the cake and ice cream.*

1 cup all-purpose flour
1 cup sugar
½ teaspoon baking soda
¼ teaspoon ground cinnamon (optional)

⅓ cup margarine or butter
¼ cup water
**3 tablespoons unsweetened cocoa
    powder**
¼ cup buttermilk or sour milk*
1 beaten egg
½ teaspoon vanilla
¼ cup finely chopped walnuts

Vanilla ice cream

1   Grease two 1-pint straight-sided, wide-mouth canning jars; line the bottom of each jar with waxed paper. Set aside.

2   In a small bowl stir together flour, sugar, baking soda, and cinnamon, if desired. Set aside.

3   In a medium saucepan combine margarine or butter, water, and cocoa powder; heat and stir till margarine is melted and mixture is well combined. Remove from heat; stir in flour mixture. Add buttermilk or sour milk, egg, and vanilla; beat by hand till smooth. Stir in nuts.

4   Pour mixture into the prepared canning jars. Cover the jars tightly with greased foil. Place the jars in a 3½-, 4-, or 5-quart crockery cooker.

5   Cover; cook on high-heat setting for 2 ¾ to 3 hours or till cakes spring back when touched and a long wooden toothpick inserted near the centers comes out clean. Remove jars from cooker; cool 10 minutes.

6   To serve, unmold cakes; discard waxed paper. Serve warm or cool with ice cream. Makes 8 servings.

*Note To make sour milk, use 1 tablespoon *lemon juice* or *vinegar* plus enough whole milk to make 1 cup. Stir together and let stand 5 minutes before using.

Per serving: 393 calories, 6 g protein, 53 g carbohydrate, 18 g total fat (6 g saturated), 56 mg cholesterol, 233 mg sodium, 174 mg potassium

Pumpkin Bread

Serve round slices of this bread with soft-style cream cheese.

½ **cup all-purpose flour**
¾ **teaspoon baking powder**
½ **teaspoon pumpkin pie spice**

¼ **cup packed brown sugar**
1 **tablespoon cooking oil**
1 **egg**
¼ **cup canned pumpkin**
2 **tablespoons raisins or dried currants,**
    finely chopped or dried cherries
    or cranberries, snipped

1 Grease two ½-pint straight-sided wide mouth canning jars well; flour the greased jars. Set aside.

2 In a small bowl combine flour, baking powder, and pumpkin pie spice.

3 In a medium mixing bowl combine brown sugar and oil; beat till well combined. Beat in egg. Add pumpkin; mix well. Add flour mixture. Beat just till combined. Stir in raisins or other dried fruit.

4 Pour mixture into the prepared canning jars. Cover the jars tightly with greased foil. Place the jars in a 3½- or 4-quart crockery cooker.

5 Cover; cook on high-heat setting for 1½ to 1¾ hours or till a wooden toothpick inserted near the centers comes out clean. Remove jars from cooker; cool 10 minutes. Carefully remove bread from jars. Cool completely on a wire rack before cutting. Makes 2 loaves (6 servings per loaf).

Per serving: *58 calories, 1 g protein, 10 g carbohydrate, 2 g total fat (0 g saturated), 18 mg cholesterol, 9 mg sodium, 49 mg potassium*

Boston Brown Bread

Great served with a baked-bean casserole or a main-dish salad.

½ **cup whole wheat flour**
¼ **cup all-purpose flour**
¼ **cup cornmeal**
½ **teaspoon baking powder**
¼ **teaspoon baking soda**
⅛ **teaspoon salt**

1 **beaten egg**
¾ **cup buttermilk or sour milk (see note, page 137)**
¼ **cup molasses**
2 **tablespoons sugar**
2 **teaspoons cooking oil**
2 **tablespoons raisins, finely chopped**

½ **cup warm water**

1 In a mixing bowl stir together whole wheat flour, all-purpose flour, cornmeal, baking powder, baking soda, and salt.

2 In a small bowl combine egg, buttermilk or sour milk, molasses, sugar, and oil. Add egg mixture to flour mixture, stirring just till combined. Stir in raisins.

3 Pour mixture into 2 well-greased 1-pint straight-sided wide-mouth canning jars; cover the jars tightly with foil. Set jars in a 4-, 5-, or 6-quart crockery cooker. Pour the ½ cup warm water into the cooker around the jars.

4 Cover; cook on high-heat setting about 2 hours or till a wooden toothpick inserted near the center comes out clean. Remove jars from cooker; cool 10 minutes. Carefully remove bread from jars. Cool completely on a rack before cutting. Makes 2 loaves (8 servings per loaf).

Per serving: 64 calories, 2 g protein, 12 g carbohydrate, 1 g total fat (0 g saturated), 14 mg cholesterol, 54 mg sodium, 96 mg potassium

Traditional Mincemeat

*Serve warm mincemeat over ice cream or use it in your
favorite recipes for mincemeat pie and muffins. Excellent apple variety
choices include Jonathan, Rome, and Golden Delicious.*

¾ **pound boneless beef chuck or round
    rump roast**
2 **pounds cooking apples, peeled, cored,
    and chopped (about 6 cups)**
1¼ **cups dark raisins**
1¼ **cups light raisins**
1 **cup currants**
⅓ **cup diced candied citron**
⅓ **cup diced mixed candied fruits and
    peels**
2 **tablespoons quick-cooking tapioca**
2 **tablespoons margarine or butter**

1 **cup sugar**
¾ **cup apple juice**
½ **cup dry sherry**
¼ **cup brandy**
¼ **cup molasses**
2 **teaspoons ground cinnamon**
1 **teaspoon ground nutmeg**
1 **teaspoon ground mace**
⅛ **teaspoon pepper**

1 Trim fat from meat; chop meat. In a
3½-, 4-, or 5-quart crockery cooker combine
chopped meat, apples, dark raisins, light
raisins, currants, citron, candied fruits and
peels, tapioca, and margarine or butter.

2 Add sugar, apple juice, sherry, brandy,
molasses, cinnamon, nutmeg, mace, and
pepper. Stir well.

3 Cover; cook on low-heat setting for 8 to
10 hours or on high-heat setting for 4 to 5
hours. Skim off fat.

4 Divide mincemeat into 1-, 2-, or 4-cup
portions. Use immediately. (Or, place into
freezer containers. Seal and label. Freeze
up to 3 months. Thaw frozen mincemeat
in the refrigerator overnight before using.)
Makes about 8 cups mincemeat.

*Per cup: 575 calories, 13 g protein, 116 g carbohy-
drate, 7 g total fat (2 g saturated), 31 mg cholesterol,
65 mg sodium, 824 mg potassium*

Index

Nutrition Analysis

Keep track of your daily nutrition needs by using the information we provide at the end of each recipe. We've analyzed the nutrition content of each recipe serving for you. When a recipe gives an ingredient substitution, we used the first choice in the analysis. If it makes a range of servings (such as 4 to 6), we used the smallest number. Ingredients listed as optional weren't included in the calculations.

Index

Metric Cooking Hints

By making a few conversions, cooks in Australia, Canada, and the United Kingdom can use the recipes in *Better Homes and Gardens® Crockery Cookbook* with confidence. The charts on this page provide a guide for converting measurements from the U.S. customary system, which is used throughout this book, to the imperial and metric systems. There also is a conversion table for oven temperatures to accommodate the differences in oven calibrations.

Volume and Weight: Americans traditionally use cup measures for liquid and solid ingredients. The chart (top right) shows the approximate imperial and metric equivalents. If you are accustomed to weighing solid ingredients, here are some helpful approximate equivalents.
● 1 cup butter, caster sugar, or rice = 8 ounces = about 250 grams
● 1 cup flour = 4 ounces = about 125 grams
● 1 cup icing sugar = 5 ounces = about 150 grams
Spoon measures are used for smaller amounts of ingredients. Although the size of the tablespoon varies slightly among countries, for practical purposes and for recipes in this book, a straight substitution is all that's necessary.
Measurements made using cups or spoons should always be level, unless stated otherwise.

Product Differences: Most of the ingredients called for in the recipes in this book are available in English-speaking countries. However, some are known by different names. Here are some common American ingredients and their possible counterparts:
● Sugar is granulated or caster sugar.
● Powdered sugar is icing sugar.
● All-purpose flour is plain household flour or white flour. When self-rising flour is used in place of all-purpose flour in a recipe that calls for leavening, omit the leavening agent (baking soda or baking powder) and salt.
● Light corn syrup is golden syrup.
● Cornstarch is cornflour.
● Baking soda is bicarbonate of soda.
● Vanilla is vanilla essence.

Useful Equivalents

⅛ teaspoon = 0.5 ml	⅔ cup = 5 fluid ounces = 150 ml
¼ teaspoon = 1 ml	¾ cup = 6 fluid ounces = 175 ml
½ teaspoon = 2 ml	1 cup = 8 fluid ounces = 250 ml
1 teaspoon = 5 ml	2 cups = 1 pint
¼ cup = 2 fluid ounces = 50 ml	2 pints = 1 litre
⅓ cup = 3 fluid ounces = 75 ml	½ inch = 1 centimetre
½ cup = 4 fluid ounces = 125 ml	1 inch = 2 centimetres

Baking Pan Sizes

American	Metric
8x1½-inch round baking pan	20x4-centimetre sandwich or cake tin
9x1½-inch round baking pan	23x3.5-centimetre sandwich or cake
11x7x1½-inch baking pan	28x18x4-centimetre baking pan
13x9x2-inch baking pan	32.5x23x5-centimetre baking pan
2-quart rectangular baking dish	30x19x5-centimetre baking pan
15x10x1-inch baking pan	38x25.5x2.5-centimetre baking pan (Swiss roll tin)
9-inch pie plate	22x4- or 23x4-centimetre pie plate
7- or 8-inch springform pan	18- or 20-centimetre springform or loose-bottom cake tin
9x5x3-inch loaf pan	23x13x6-centimetre or 2-pound narrow loaf pan or paté tin
1½-quart casserole	1.5-litre casserole
2-quart casserole	2-litre casserole

Oven Temperature Equivalents

Fahrenheit Setting	Celsius Setting*	Gas Setting
300°F	150°C	Gas Mark 2
325°F	160°C	Gas Mark 3
350°F	180°C	Gas Mark 4
375°F	190°C	Gas Mark 5
400°F	200°C	Gas Mark 6
425°F	220°C	Gas Mark 7
450°F	230°C	Gas Mark 8
Broil		Grill

Electric and gas ovens may be calibrated using Celsius. However, increase the Celsius setting 10 to 20 degrees when cooking above 160°C with an electric oven. For convection or forced-air ovens (gas or electric), lower the temperature setting 10°C when cooking at all heat levels.